For Uncle Pete

God bless!
Donna-Marie

Our Lady of Fatima

100 years of stories, prayers, and devotions

• • •

Donna-Marie Cooper O'Boyle

servant
AN IMPRINT OF
FRANCISCAN MEDIA
Cincinnati, Ohio

LIBRARY OF CONGRESS CATALOGING-IN-PUBLICATION DATA
Names: O'Boyle, Donna-Marie Cooper, author.
Title: Our Lady of Fatima : one hundred years of stories, prayers, and devotions / Donna-Marie Cooper O'Boyle.
Description: Cincinnati, OH : Servant, [2017] | Includes bibliographical references and index.
Identifiers: LCCN 2016059144 | ISBN 9781632531582 (paperback)
Subjects: LCSH: Fatima, Our Lady of. | Mary, Blessed Virgin, Saint—Prayers and devotions. | BISAC: RELIGION / Christian Life / Inspirational. | RELIGION / Christianity / Catholic. | RELIGION / Christian Theology / Mariology.
Classification: LCC BT660.F3 O26 2017 | DDC 232.91/70946945—dc23
LC record available at https://lccn.loc.gov/2016059144

Cover and book design by Mark Sullivan

Published by Servant
an imprint of Franciscan Media
28 W. Liberty St.
Cincinnati, OH 45202
www.FranciscanMedia.org

Printed in the United States of America.
Printed on acid-free paper.
17 18 19 20 21 5 4 3 2 1

With great love, this book is dedicated to all of my children:
Justin, Chaldea, Jessica, Joseph, and Mary-Catherine and to my
grandson Shepherd James. It is dedicated also to the
Immaculate Heart of Mary, Our Lady of Fatima,
our Queen of Heaven and Earth,
who is the cause of our joy!

Contents

The year 2017 will be a great Marian Year, since we have waited and prepared for one hundred years to carry out the requests Our Lady made of us at Fatima a century ago. She promised that her triumph would come when enough people would do as she requested. This would bring world peace through the conversion of many sinners. We see how dangerous the world situation is in terms of potential violence: war, even nuclear war; terrorism; the loss of respect for human life from its conception to natural death. At the same time, how many people have abandoned any faith in God. Our Lady said to the three shepherd children, Lucia, Francisco, and Jacinta: "Many souls are lost from God because there is no one to pray and offer sacrifices for their conversion." We must all respond to Our Lady's request if there is to be world peace.

In order for us to do this, we must know the message of Our Lady clearly, so that we can respond wholeheartedly to it. Pope Emeritus Benedict XVI put it this way: "To be an 'apostle' of Our Lady: LEARN the message of Fatima, LIVE the message of Fatima, and SPREAD the message of Fatima." This book is a wonderful source of information for those who know little about Fatima as well as a renewal of inspiration for those who already know much.

As reflected in the book's title, Donna-Marie used stories. There are stories of the effect the Fatima message has had on peoples' lives, plus fascinating stories of St. Mother Teresa of Calcutta (whom Donna-Marie knew so well) and other Church figures. Donna-Marie presents the history of all the apparitions of the Angel of Peace (1916), of Our Blessed Lady at the Cova (1917), and the apparitions later on at

Ponte Vedra, Spain (1925), where Our Lady requested the Five First Saturdays devotion and at Tuy, Spain (1929), where she requested that the pope along with the bishops of the world consecrate Russia to her lmmaculate Heart. These will give you much to ponder of Our Lady's requests and how to fulfill them.

Fr. Andrew Apostoli, CFR
Saint Leopold Friary

Fatima is undoubtedly the most prophetic of modern apparitions.[1]

—Congregation of the Doctrine of the Faith

Ninety-nine years ago, Our Blessed Mother's great love for her children was manifested in her appearance to three young peasant children on the rocky hillside in Fatima, Portugal. During this, her first appearance, the Blessed Virgin Mary asked the children to pray the rosary for the conversion of sinners. Mary specifically instructed, "Pray the rosary every day, in order to obtain peace for the world, and the end of the war."

As I type these words, my heart is bursting to share this important and most essential message given us from heaven. I have always loved the Blessed Mother and feel very fortunate to have been raised in the Catholic faith, knowing about our Mother in Heaven. My dear friend and spiritual mother, St. Teresa of Calcutta, whom I was privileged to know for ten years and who was very close to the Blessed Mother, encouraged me to turn to Mary often with this simple prayer.

"Mary, Mother of Jesus, be Mother to me now."

Mother Teresa often prodded me to "bring others to Jesus through Mary." In the almost two dozen letters she wrote to me, she frequently mentioned Mother Mary. In one she said, "Pray to Our Lady—pray the rosary very fervently, cling to Our Lady. She will surely lead you to Jesus to know His will for you." A couple of years ago, I had the most amazing and beautiful dream on the night of the Feast of the Immaculate Heart of Mary, in which St. Teresa of Calcutta appeared to me and very clearly asked me if I was offering my sufferings and sacrifices. I exuberantly told her, "Yes!" But immediately after I uttered that word of affirmation to her, I was made to know that there is so much more to offer.

Recently, I took out my notebook filled with Mother Teresa's letters, which had been lovingly typed to me on an old typewriter. Some letters of the alphabet were typed so gloriously askew, a sign of the age of the typewriter and of the faithful and frail woman whose holy passion inspired her to sit and type away, long after her duties of the day were completed. Every one of Mother Teresa's letters to me pierced my heart with a tender love that cannot be articulated. In seeing them again, some took on new meaning and implication as I read them slowly, meditating upon the words.

In October 1987, she wrote, "Please continue praying and offering your sufferings for our Mother—she needs it most now." All these years later, I understand more clearly what Mother Teresa was asking of me.

As my spiritual mother's heart overflowed with passion to encourage me to know the Mother, so my heart longs to encourage you through the story of Our Lady of Fatima. I pray that as you read through the history and heavenly messages of one of the most popular and prophetic of all Marian apparitions in Church history, you will grow closer to the Blessed Mother who always leads souls closer to her Son Jesus. I am praying to the Blessed Mother and asking the intercession of Blessed Francisco, Blessed Jacinta, and Lucia to pray for me as I write this book and for each person who will read this book so that they will be deeply transformed and moved by grace!

I hope and pray that you, dear reader, will become more prayerful and interested in doing your part to bring about the conversions of sinners through your prayers and offerings of sufferings and mortifications for the glory of God. This is what Our Lady of Fatima has asked of us.

Jesus and his Mother Mary await generous souls who are willing to make reparation for all those who are in danger of losing their souls to hell. Will you be a generous soul?

Let us pray to the Immaculate Heart of Mary for all of the graces that we need to be a brilliant light and a holy comfort to others each and every day in this darkened and sometimes frightening world. Don't forget to offer your sufferings to God and to make sacrifices to save souls.

Queen of the Most Holy Rosary, Our Lady of Fatima, our dear Mother in Heaven, please pray for us. Please help our world! We are comforted knowing that your Immaculate Heart will triumph.

> Yours in prayer and the love of the Holy Family,
> Donna-Marie Cooper O'Boyle
> May 13, 2016
> Feast of Our Lady of Fatima

Chapter One

FATIMA, PORTUGAL, YESTERDAY AND TODAY

The appeal of the Lady of the message of Fatima is so deeply rooted in the Gospel and the whole of Tradition that *the Church feels that the message imposes a commitment on her.*[1]

—St. John Paul II

For nearly a hundred years, memories of Fatima processions and devotions have been etched upon the hearts of many. The Miracle of the Sun at Fatima has been told and retold, even captured in movie form. And yet, there are many who have never heard the story of the apparitions, visions, and miracles of the Blessed Mother that occurred in the small village of Fatima.

When he was pope, St. John Paul II made a special pilgrimage to Portugal to commemorate the first anniversary of the assassination attempt on his life. The Holy Father visited the Shrine of Our Lady of Fatima on May 13, 1982, the second day of his pilgrimage, which was the sixty-fifth anniversary of Our Lady's first apparition there. During the homily of his Mass the Holy Father said:

If the Church has accepted the message of Fatima, it is above all because that message contains a truth and a call whose basic content is the truth and the call of the Gospel itself.

"Repent, and believe in the gospel" (Mark 1:15): these are the first words that the Messiah addressed to humanity. The message of Fatima is, in its basic nucleus, a call to conversion and repentance, as in the Gospel. This call was uttered at the beginning of the twentieth century, and it was thus addressed particularly to this present century. The Lady of the message seems to have read with special insight the "signs of the times," the signs of our time.[2]

Fatima Yesterday

The name Fatima hints at its multicultural origins, including the traditions of other faiths, including Islam. It is believed that Mohammed had a daughter named Fatima, for whom many Muslim girls are still named.

According to tradition, in 1158 a powerful Muslim prince named Alacer de Sol was captured by the crusader Goncalo Hermingues. Goncalo asked the prince for his daughter's hand in marriage. His daughter, Fatima, then became a Christian and was baptized at Oureana, which gave its name to the nearby town of Ourem.

The princess died young and her grieving husband decided to retreat from the world to become a monk, entering the Cistercian monastery at Alcobaca. Not too long after, a small priory was started in the neighboring mountainside. Brother Goncalo was sent to live there and took with him the mortal remains of his beloved spouse. Tradition holds that this place took on Fatima's name and has kept it to this day.

Centuries later, in 1385, the existence of the nation of Portugal was threatened by war. Under the leadership of Dom Nuno Alvares Pereira, who had a strong devotion to the Mother of God, the nation was eventually delivered.

Archbishop Fulton Sheen says, "I believe that the Blessed Virgin chose to be known as 'Our Lady of Fatima' as a pledge and a sign of hope to the Muslim people, and as an assurance that they, who show her so much respect, will one day accept her Divine Son too!" Fr. Andrew Apostoli, CFR, one of the world's leading Fatima experts and vice-postulator of Archbishop Sheen's cause for canonization, wrote, "[Archbishop Sheen] held that Our Lady did not appear in the only place in Portugal with a Muslim name (Fatima was named after a Muslim princess who converted to the Catholic faith), simply to convert Russia. She came also for the conversion of the Moslem people because, as he believed, unless a great number of Muslims were converted, there would never be peace in the world."[3]

In 1917, the First World War was at its height. Lenin had arrived in Russia in April of that year. The Bolshevik Revolution occurred in October and November, and the atheistic Communist movement was gaining momentum. The war had a death grip on the world, and there was little hope of peace returning anytime soon.

Like so many small towns in Europe during those tumultuous days, the unassuming agricultural town of Fatima was surrounded by the horrors of that Great War. The destruction and violence had never been so far-reaching, nor so intimately felt by citizens who had always lived quiet lives on farms and in fields. Such devastation shook the faith of many, including the shepherds and farmers living in Fatima at the time. But then, in the midst of humanity's chaos, something extraordinary happened. The Queen of Heaven woke up the sleepy village, appearing to three peasant children to deliver her message of penance, prayer, and peace.

The Little Visionaries: Lucia, Francisco, and Jacinta

The Lord often surprises us in his choice of messenger. He uses the humble, the weak, the small. Often, he chooses children to bear his message of hope and peace. In Fatima, he chose Lucia dos Santos, age ten, and her younger cousins, brother and sister Francisco, nine, and Jacinta Marto, seven. These three simple yet faithful children, all from Catholic farm families, were good children from humble backgrounds. Yet, by God's grace, their lives—and ours—were forever changed. Because of heaven's designs on their hearts, they all experienced deeper conversions of heart as we shall see as the Fatima story unfolds. We will get to these children in great detail a little later on. For now, let us look at a little history and some modern-day transforming visits to Fatima.

Fatima, Portugal, holds much Marian history. World-renowned theologian Fr. John A. Hardon, my friend and former spiritual director, explains:

> The scope of the Fatima apparitions is global. But the place and the people where these apparitions took place can be called unique in the Church's geography and history. For over a thousand years, Portugal and its citizens have looked to Mary for survival and religious freedom in a way that is quite unparalleled in the annals of Catholic Christianity. We may call this the backdrop of Fatima or, better, its proof from experience. The Portuguese are a standing witness to the Blessed Virgin's power under God to perform moral miracles in the minds and hearts of sinful human beings—provided there are enough clients of Mary to invoke her great name.[4]

A Papal History

A number of popes have been drawn to Fatima and have shown their great devotion to the Mother of God, who revealed herself there as the "Queen of the Rosary."

In honor of the twenty-fifth anniversary of the Fatima apparitions, on October 31, 1942, Pope Pius XII (1939–1958) solemnly consecrated the world to the Immaculate Heart of Mary. On May 13, 1946, his papal legate, Cardinal Masella, crowned the statue of Our Lady of Fatima on the three hundredth anniversary of the consecration of the nation of Portugal to Mary Immaculate.

On May 13, 1967, on the fiftieth anniversary of the apparitions, Pope Paul VI (1963–1978) made his own pilgrimage to Fatima. On that occasion, he published an apostolic exhortation, *Signum Magnum*, inviting "all members of the Church to consecrate themselves to Mary Immaculate and to put this pious act into concrete action in their daily lives."

Pope St. John Paul II also made a pilgrimage to Fatima. He wished to give thanks for Mary's intercession in saving his life a year earlier. He believed that the Blessed Mother guided the bullet that shot him and protected him from death. He offered Mass there on May 13, 1982, reminding the faithful that "the message of Fatima is a call to conversion and repentance, the nucleus of the message of the Gospel." He reconsecrated the world to Mary's Immaculate Heart. He encouraged everyone to pray, especially the prayer of the rosary.

The first structure to be built on the location of the apparitions (which we will discuss later) was a small archway. Soon after, the modest archway was replaced by a tiny chapel which was built over the exact spot of the apparitions. When this first chapel was destroyed by dynamite in 1922, a second chapel was built, as well as the Pavilion of the Sick.

The foundation stone for the Basilica of Our Lady of the Rosary was laid on October 13, 1928. On October 6, 1953, Cardinal Cerejeira, the patriarch of Lisbon, solemnly consecrated the structure. Fifteen altars, in honor of the original mysteries of the rosary, were positioned all along the colonnade of the Basilica. Today, hundreds of thousands of pilgrims, desiring to feel closer to the Mother of God and striving to do their part in heeding her messages, continue to descend upon the hallowed ground.

Transforming Visits
Portugal has made quite an impression on countless pilgrims who travel to the Shrine for myriad reasons. One reason is always the same—they are seeking something: an answer, a cure, a dose of hope, a time to honor Mary, some direction, an understanding of their path in life, a deeper growth in holiness, peace of heart, and more. The Fatima experience is transformative, whether it was experienced in 1917 or any time throughout the one hundred years since then.

Many pilgrims are brought deeper into their faith and gain new understanding. My friend Patty shared her own experience: "It was when I read about Fatima that I first began to understand the Eucharist—and I had been brought up in Catholic schools. But somehow it didn't click in until I saw the great honor the Angel gave to the Most Blessed Sacrament that I realized it was the Body, Blood, Soul, and Divinity of Our Lord."

Through the message of Fatima, Patty, like so many others, was drawn deeper into communion with Christ. Fatima turns our attention to what is most important. We know that Mother Mary desires to help us and draw our hearts to her own Immaculate one. Mary actually beckons to us to come and sit on her lap, to tell her our cares and our woes, to allow her to bring us closer to her Son.

Mary Mothers Us

It was her Divine Son Jesus, after all, who gave us the eminent gift of his Mother even as he was dying on the Cross: "Then he said to the disciple, 'Here is your mother'" (John 19:27). St. John Paul II reminds us, "From the time when 'the disciple took her to his own home,' the mystery *of the spiritual motherhood of Mary* has been actualized boundlessly in history. Motherhood means caring for the life of the child. Since Mary is the mother of us all, her care for the life of man is *universal.*"[5]

We can all understand the universal care of our Mother in Heaven for us or, at the very least, the longing for that spiritual motherly care in our lives. The Blessed Mother's love and care is especially healing for those whose own biological mothers were unwilling or unable to provide authentic self-giving love. Mother Mary loves us all with a pure, selfless, and steadfast motherly love. She tirelessly calls to our hearts and souls. Her utmost aim is to bring us to her Son.

Mother Mary's care is rooted in the Holy Spirit. St. John Paul

II tells us, "The care of a mother embraces her child totally. Mary's motherhood has its beginning in her motherly care for Christ. In Christ, at the foot of the cross, she accepted John, and in John she *accepted all of us totally*. Mary embraces us all with special solicitude in *the Holy Spirit*. For as we profess in our *Creed*, he is 'the giver of life.' It is he who gives the fullness of life, open towards eternity."[6]

We can come to understand the messages and reasons for Our Lady's visits in Fatima, Portugal, when we reflect on Mary's humble, loving service right from the start—at the Annunciation, at the wedding feast at Cana, and at foot of the Cross. Through her life in Scripture, we see how Mother Mary wants to protect us and draw us to her Son.

We can visit the shrine at Fatima to experience the spiritual love and care of our Mother and Queen of Heaven, just as we can also experience that same spiritual mothering within each and every Hail Mary we utter sincerely from our hearts, and with every rosary prayed. Mother Mary is right there with us, granting her graces and lovingly pushing us forth—always towards her Son Jesus, so that we will be able to continue each day to put one foot in front of the other to walk in faith.

Mary's "Dwelling Places"

St. John Paul II spoke about Mary's spiritual motherhood and her "dwelling places" during his homily when visiting Fatima on the sixty-fifth anniversary as was mentioned earlier. He was there to give thanks to her for saving his life exactly one year earlier and to celebrate her message at Fatima. He said:

> Mary's spiritual motherhood is therefore a *sharing* in the *power of the Holy Spirit*, of "the giver of life." It is the humble service of her who says of herself: "Behold, I am the handmaid of the Lord" (Luke 1:38).

In the light of the mystery of Mary's spiritual motherhood, let us seek to understand the *extraordinary message*, which began on May 13, 1917, to resound throughout the world from Fatima, continuing through October of the same year.

Mary's motherhood in our regard is manifested in a particular way in the places where she meets us: *her dwelling places*; places in which a special presence of the Mother is felt. There are many such dwelling places. They are of all kinds: from a special corner in the home or little wayside shrines adorned with an image of the Mother of God, to chapels and churches built in her honor.

However, in certain *places, the Mother's presence is felt in a particularly vivid way*. These places sometimes radiate their light over a great distance and draw people from afar. Their radiance may extend over a diocese, a whole nation, or at times over several countries and even continents. These places are *the Marian sanctuaries or shrines*.

In all these places, that unique testament of the Crucified Lord is wonderfully actualized: in them man feels that he is entrusted and confided to Mary; he goes there in order to be with her, as with his Mother, he opens his heart to her and speaks to her about everything: he "takes her to his own home," that is to say, he brings her into all his problems, which at times are difficult. His own problems and those of others. The problems of the family, of societies, of nations and of the whole of humanity.[7]

Pilgrims

Pilgrims enter the story of Fatima from the second apparition of Our Lady, in June 1917. They had heard about the first visit from the mysterious heavenly stranger and wanted to know more. They also desired to show their love to the Queen of Heaven, whom they suspected was appearing to the three humble, young shepherds. Hundreds of pilgrims traveled long distances to be a part of what was going on. They prayed on their way to the Cova da Iria (Cove of Irene, a name that comes from the Greek word meaning "peace"). After arriving, they prayed the rosary together while waiting for something to happen. Over the years, hundreds of thousands of pilgrims would come.

For nearly a century, people from all walks of life have continued to make sacrifices to experience Fatima. Many arrive with swollen feet from the long, arduous hike. Others arrive bloodied after slowly making their way on their knees upon the hard ground of the penitential path, which begins at the entrance to the Cova, to arrive at the sacred place where the Queen of Heaven appeared to the shepherd children. The pilgrims sacrifice their comfort to open their hearts to the Blessed Mother's message and peace plan for the world.

Fr. Robert J. Fox, a Fatima expert, said he was deeply touched by the humility of the pilgrims and that "there was a sense of the special presence of the Mother of God in the Cova da Iria. Enhancing that sense of the 'graces which flow in the Cova da Iria,' as Pope Pius XII explained it, was the obvious faith, love, and humility of the Portuguese pilgrims."

David Carollo, executive director for the World Apostolate of Fatima USA, told me:

> The message of Our Lady given at Fatima is a prescription for life. We must live in accord with the laws of God if we expect to have peace on this earth and in eternity. We must also repair the damage that we have inflicted on our relationship with Almighty God. Our Lady is the finest of His creation, who understands more than anyone the tragedy of separation from Him. She wants us to avoid this.

Pope John Paul II said Fatima was the greatest apparition of the twentieth century and of perhaps all time. Fr. Andrew Apostoli,

CFR, said, "Our Lady called her children to live holy lives of prayer and penance. This is missing in many people's lives today. They reject sacrifice because they're attached to the world and so cannot allow Jesus into their lives. If we follow what Our Lady is asking, we will find ourselves close to Jesus."[8]

The Revelations of Children

Why should anyone believe what is said to have happened at Fatima, Portugal, in 1916 and 1917? Can we trust the claims of three peasant children?

First of all, it's important to note that the happenings of Fatima have been scrutinized and examined completely by the Catholic Church and have been found to be authentic and completely true. However, though they are entirely approved by the Church, they are still considered to be private revelations, distinguished from the public revelation contained in Sacred Scripture and Sacred Tradition.

Servant of God Fr. John Hardon, SJ, explained the difference between public revelation and authentic private revelation this way: He said public revelation means "truths revealed [that] are necessary for the salvation and sanctification of the human race. All other authentic revelations, although supernatural, are called private because they contain nothing which is not already contained in the Bible and revealed Tradition."

Though we are not obliged to believe in private revelation, Fr. Hardon went on to say that these messages revealed by the great mystics of the Church and apparitions like that of Fatima have a purpose: "to recall what had already been revealed up to apostolic times and to reaffirm what needs to be believed and put into practice in times like ours. Surely ours is a period of trial, and some would say it is the most critical age in the history of Christianity."[9]

Like the children who witnessed the miracle at Fatima, we are given an opportunity to believe and to learn. The Church, of course, guides us through its own scrutiny and acceptance of the revelation of the children, but it is up to us to take the words of Our Lady of Fatima into our hearts.

Fr. Andrew Apostoli, CFR: Vocation to Priesthood Inspired by Fatima

Fr. Andrew Apostoli, CFR, was inspired by the message of Fatima as a child. He vividly remembers watching the 1952 movie *The Miracle of Our Lady of Fatima*, which made a great impression on him. He grew up praying the family rosary and recalled, "I think it was while saying those rosaries that there was a stirring in my heart to become a priest." Fr. Apostoli was ordained a priest in 1967 by Bishop Fulton Sheen in the Rochester, New York, diocese. He later joined with Fr. Benedict Groeschel (now deceased) and six other Capuchin friars to found the Franciscan Friars of the Renewal. Fr. Apostoli is host of EWTN's *Sunday Night Prime.*

Fr. Apostoli has been to Fatima about ten times since his first trip in 1985. In a January 2016 interview with the *Catholic World Report,* Fr. Apostoli spoke about his interest in the message of Fatima. He said, "Over the years my interest has grown immensely, especially considering the sad state of our world today. It was Pope St. John Paul who said that the Church was facing her greatest spiritual struggle in her history, and most Catholics are not even aware that there is a struggle going on." He continued, "There is an evil out there that desires the total destruction of Christian civilization; that's why the message of Fatima is so important."

In an *EWTN News* interview, Fr. Apostoli spoke about Our Lady of Fatima and how through her apparitions, the Blessed Mother gave the world the sure recipe for peace. He said, "Our Lady said that the rosary can stop wars, and can bring world peace. We have to do what she said, and live good lives." He added, "There's no other plan from heaven that's so specific, for what we're going through now. She [the Blessed Mother] spelled it out. Prayer, penance, the First Saturdays' devotion—and live a good, holy life. That's the answer."[10]

Fr. Apostoli explained to me why Fatima remains a very popular and meaningful pilgrimage site to him personally. "I think when you realize the Blessed Mother was there...it does inspire you. If you would compare Fatima and Lourdes, Lourdes is more important as far as the place—the bathing in the water there—Our Lady wanting people to come and so on." He continued, "However, Fatima, besides being a place where Our Lady came, it's very devotional. But, its importance is in the message [the Blessed Mother] gave for our time—the message for peace through the salvation of souls."

Why do pilgrims continue to flock to the site of these apparitions, even today? Fr. Apostoli explained that Fatima is "a place made holy by her coming—people feel a sense of her presence." He added, "As Pope John Paul II said when he made the consecration in 1984, 'Fatima is more important now than it was in 1917.' And it's even more important now in 2016 than when he said that in 1984."

A Silent Retreat at Fatima

As we learned from St. John Paul II, "In certain *places, the Mother's presence is felt in a particularly vivid way.*" Fr. Michael J. Russo, pastor of Our Lady of Fatima parish in Lafayette, Louisiana, can certainly attest to that statement. In addition to feeling the Blessed Mother's loving presence to at least some degree at the Marian parishes he has served, Fr. Russo, who was ordained on May 28, 1989, in St. Peter's Basilica by St. John Paul II, considers himself deeply blessed to have felt the Blessed Mother's presence at Fatima.

Fr. Russo recalled, "Perhaps Fatima is my favorite Marian spot because the story is so real." Recalling his very first visit to Fatima in 1987 as a seminarian in Rome, Fr. Russo described his pilgrimage to Fatima during Easter break. "At that time, Francisco and Jacinta's brother, John, was still living. I remember him having the most beautiful eyes. Sr. Lucia mentions him in the August 1917 apparition," he said.

Where did this love for the Blessed Mother begin for Fr. Russo? His fascination with Our Lady of Fatima started as a young boy. He tells the story:

> My dad's best friend lived in a city about an hour and a half away from my hometown. Occasionally, we would visit over the weekend and would attend Holy Mass at my dad's friend's church. The name of the church was Our Lady of Fatima. I remember the first time I walked into the church and saw the beautiful massive stained glass window of the Miracle of the Sun. From that moment, my heart was captivated, made all the more exciting when I learned that Our Lady had actually appeared to young children in her Fatima apparitions—children who were my age at the time. In the world of child-like imagination, I longed for Our Lady to appear to me. After all, she had appeared to young children at Fatima. Years later, in God's Divine Providence, I would be named the pastor of this same church, with its stained glass window that ignited my heart years earlier as a young boy.

Fr. Russo's regular Fatima visits began in late November 2004 when he decided to spend a thirty-day retreat at Fatima in silent prayer. After fifteen years of priestly ministry, Fr. Russo had arranged to take a four-month sabbatical—three months spent in a study program in Rome where he had made his theological studies for the priesthood, and one month dedicated to silent prayer at the shrine in Fatima.

"I was determined to take full advantage of this month of prayer. I stayed at the Carmelite Retreat House, right off of the Cova da Iria where Pope John Paul II would stay during his visits to Fatima. It is the perfect spot," Fr. Russo recalled.

Our Lady took very good care of Fr. Russo during his time of silence and reflection. "Knowing the European custom of eating the evening meal very late, I arranged to have my meals much earlier, and in silence," Fr. Russo explained. "The sweet lady in charge of the kitchen, informed that I was a priest from the United States, gave extra special treatment to me."

Fr. Russo committed to a prayer and sacred reading regimen, to nourish his heart and soul, and an exercise regimen, to take care of his body. "While on sabbatical, I prayed four hours a day, read intensively, including the entire New Testament, and spoke to no one," he said.

Well, there was one exception. While checking out the surroundings during a casual stroll in his early days at Fatima, Fr. Russo came upon a gym. He decided to join the gym for the month he would be in Fatima. Throughout his stay, Fr. Russo would greet the young man who managed the gym. "Each afternoon, after lunch, I would make my way to the gym, still determined to talk very little in order to keep my contemplative spirit. On my last day, I decided to tell the gym manager that I was a priest from the United States."

Fr. Russo received an unexpected response. "Oh Father, I figured that out on your first day here." They both smiled.

Throughout the thirty days, Fr. Russo took all that he could of Fatima into his heart. "My time at Fatima was everything I had hoped it to be…," he recalled. "I loved being at the actual apparition spot, immersed in prayer and integrating the important messages Our Lady gave to the world at this exact spot—prophetic messages that I would actually live to see unfold."

Fr. Russo visited each precise location and pondered its amazing history. "Here is where the children saw the vision of hell and first heard of the rise of Communism and the great persecution of the Church that would come. Here, at this spot, is where Our Lady came down from heaven to speak to us as a Mother. The thought of it all was overwhelming," he shared. "The silence helped me to experience her motherly presence."

Fr. Russo didn't realize it at the time that he was there in silence, drinking in all of the graces, but the Blessed Mother would soon reveal to him a specific plan for his life. "I know now, looking back," he said, "that during that one month at Fatima, Our Lady was preparing me to be the pastor of her church here in Lafayette…during the time of the one hundredth anniversary of her apparitions to the world. It is a tremendous gift to me as a priest." Fr. Russo continues to feel privileged to be blessed with the opportunity to help guide his parishioners ever closer to Jesus through Mary.

Everything came together in that holy place for Fr. Russo—aiding and preparing him for his future position as pastor at a parish dedicated to Our Lady of Fatima. "In addition to the moments of deep contemplation, how could I forget the beautiful liturgies at the Shrine? I particularly recall the Solemn Mass of the Solemnity of the Immaculate Conception on December 8. There were so many families from all over Portugal who came to the Shrine on that special day to be with Our Lady. It was encouraging to see the love and devotion of the Portuguese people for their patroness."

When Fr. Russo's sabbatical ended, he traveled to Rome to spend Christmas before returning to parish life. "I [received]…Holy Communion from the Pope [John Paul II] during the Christmas Midnight Mass, a Mass I had always attended when a student in Rome. It was Pope John Paul II's last liturgy in St. Peter's Basilica; four months later he would be dead."

Since his sabbatical, Fr. Russo has returned to Fatima at least three times on various pilgrimages. He plans to return in 2017 "as a way of commemorating the one hundredth anniversary of Our Lady's visit."

A Lifelong Interest

Colin B. Donovan, STL, vice president for theology at EWTN, remembers first learning about Our Lady of Fatima from the nuns when he was in kindergarten in the 1950s. He said, "I don't really remember *not* knowing about Fatima or *not* being interested, at some level."

The Fatima message stayed with Donovan throughout his life. In an interview for this book, he recalled, "The most important impression I had at the time, and from Catholic devotional practice generally, was that we can turn to Our Lady using the rosary for our needs, and I did and I do." Donovan believed the authenticity of the messages of Fatima from an early age. Reflecting on his straightforward beliefs, he said, "I don't recall ever having to be convinced about Fatima, as it was uncontroversial that it was simply true that the Mother of God had appeared, made certain predictions, worked a great miracle, and recruited us anew to help her and her Son in the conversion of the world."

In the 1980s Donovan took up residence in Fatima. "I had the privilege to live in Fatima for fourteen months in discernment and formation for a religious community. It gave me the opportunity to deepen my appreciation of Fatima and its message and become personally acquainted with the locations associated with it," he explained. Donovan had also visited other Marian shrines but was impressed with the prayerful atmosphere of Fatima.

He said, "Having visited Guadalupe, Lourdes, La Salette, as well as holy places in Italy, Spain, and the Holy Land, the thing which impressed me most about Fatima is a prayerful, almost austere, atmosphere, gifts shops and the hustle and bustle of pilgrims notwithstanding." He attributes this atmosphere to the geographic isolation and relative poverty of Portugal, as well as the way the message is lived out among the pilgrims, something he experienced personally in the 1980s and 1990s. For him, it is a holy place, a "dwelling place" to encounter the transforming presence of God.

Mother Teresa and Our Lady of Fatima

St. Teresa of Calcutta had a profound love for the Blessed Mother and even received locutions and visions from her when she was starting the religious order of the Missionaries of Charity to take care of the poorest of the poor all around the globe.

Our Lady told Mother Teresa back in 1947: "Fear not, teach [the people] to say the Rosary, the family Rosary—and all will be well. Fear not—Jesus and I will be with you and with your children."[11]

Mother Teresa could always be seen with a rosary in hand or hanging from her sari when her hands were occupied in service. Mother Teresa was very connected to the messages of Our Lady of Fatima. As a Loreto Sister, she created a little shrine to Our Lady of Fatima. The patroness of the Missionaries of Charity is the Immaculate Heart of Mary. Mother Teresa promoted the message of Fatima to the poor and needy that she served.

In an interview, Fr. Brian Kolodiejchuk, postulator of Mother Teresa's cause for canonization, said, "In 1947, when she [Mother Teresa] was waiting for Archbishop Perrier of Calcutta to give his OK for her to begin her work in Calcutta, in one of the letters, she spoke of Our Lady of Fatima and said, 'We will do her work in the slums.' So it was very explicit that they would take the message of Our Lady of Fatima, at least amongst the Catholics in Calcutta, to promote that message."[12]

Author David Scott in his book *The Love That Made Mother Teresa* said, "On the day Mother Teresa died, her sisters laid her in state beneath Our Lady of Fatima, a statue of the Blessed Mother depicted as she appeared to the children at Fatima. It was fitting in a way that no one could have known at the time."[13] Scott elaborated on Mother Teresa's connection with Fatima and the consecration of Russia to the Immaculate Heart of Mary:

> Few knew that she had been guided all these years by apparitions and a voice heard one summer long ago. And few knew that she was of the world to show Mary's love for her children, to show us the blessed fruit of Mary's womb, Jesus. We can now see that Mother Teresa was among the first fruits of the pope's consecration of the world to Mary's Immaculate Heart. The child called Gonxha, "flower bud," became the first bud of new Christian life, flowering from the century's bloody soil of wars, famines, and persecutions.
>
> Mother Teresa had followed the call of the gospel and done all that had been asked of her by Jesus and Mary in those 1946 visions. They were visions for which her whole life had prepared her—and visions that she lived out for all generations to come. Kept secret during her lifetime, these things have been disclosed to us now in the early days of the new millennium so that we might understand more fully the meaning of Mother Teresa and the revolution of love that God was working in our midst.[14]

Mother Teresa loved to give blessed Miraculous Medals to those she met. The Miraculous Medal wins extraordinary graces for those who wear them and pray for Mary's graces, intercession, and help. The medals were first introduced by St. Catherine Laboure in 1830. St. Catherine received visions from the Blessed Mother at the Daughters of Charity of St. Vincent de Paul motherhouse in Paris. The Blessed

Mother instructed Sister Catherine to have medals made which were first called the Medal of the Immaculate Conception and later acquired the name Miraculous Medal due to the miraculous occurrences involving the medals. In 1832 with the approval of the archbishop, the medals were struck and distributed around Paris. The words "O Mary, conceived without sin, pray for us who have recourse to thee" are stamped on the medal at the Blessed Mother's request.

The Miraculous Medal devotion spread with incredible speed and intensity. Many graces were manifested as miracles of peace, health, and prosperity.

In addition to gifting the Miraculous Medals to people, Mother Teresa also placed the blessed medals in specific areas, asking the Blessed Mother to work her miracles in those locations. One time, Mother Teresa used a medal in hope of securing a piece of property for one of her homes. Miraculously, after Mother Teresa placed the medal on the property in Dublin, Ireland, she soon received a donation for the exact amount she needed to purchase the land.

Other times, Mother Teresa would gently rub the medal on someone experiencing hurt or pain and ask the Blessed Mother to help. I have since taken up Mother Teresa's practice of giving out blessed Miraculous Medals and have been fortunate to do it all over the world. I have watched amazing transformations take place before my eyes. Eager to share about the history and amazing graces of the Miraculous Medal, I wrote a book about it titled *The Miraculous Medal: Stories, Prayers, and Devotions*.

Mother Teresa had a deep desire to get a blessed Miraculous Medal into the Kremlin on the exact day and time that Pope John Paul II would consecrate the world to the Immaculate Heart of Mary!

Not many know that Mother Teresa desired to work and pray for the conversion of Russia. This aspect of Mother Teresa's life was revealed by the Most Reverend Pavol Hnilica, the Slovak bishop who was Mother Teresa's friend for thirty-three years and who collaborated with her on many initiatives. Bishop Hnilica was also fortunate to have communication and visits with Sister Lucia.

Bishop Hnilica recalled, "For years, Mother Teresa wished to travel to Russia with her nuns to witness to the Christian faith… she managed to fulfill her wish at the end of the 1980s with the help of Raisa Gorbachev, the wife of Mikhail Gorbachev, the then Soviet president."

In an interview with *Messenger of St. Anthony*, Bishop Hnilica explained one of the reasons Mother Teresa felt close to the Russian people. "Mother Teresa was born in Skopje, in Kosovo, in 1910, and so she was of Slavic blood. This is why she considered herself almost related to the Russian population and suffered greatly whenever she heard that Soviet Communism persecuted mercilessly any form of religion."

Combine Mother Teresa's heartfelt closeness to the Russian people and her deep devotion to the Blessed Mother with her message of Fatima, and you have a great inspiration.

"We often spoke of Russia," Bishop Hnilica recalled. "Mother Teresa was very familiar with what the Virgin had said during the apparitions in Fatima, and that an atheist ideology would arise, spreading errors world-wide, but that in the end 'Russia would be converted and [her] Immaculate Heart would triumph,'" Bishop Hnilica said.

After a visit with Sister Lucia, Bishop Hnilica felt very impacted by the "Russia element" of the Fatima message and felt compelled to convey it to Mother Teresa. In his interview with *Messenger of St. Anthony*, he said:

> One day, on returning from Fatima where I had met Sister Lucia,
> I recounted to Mother Teresa what this famous seer had told me.

I paused on a detail which had struck me, namely, that the Virgin of Fatima, in various apparitions, the official ones in 1917 and the private ones before Sister Lucia in the years that followed, had expressed an interest in Russia a good 22 times. 'This insistence,' I said to Mother Teresa, 'is proof of extraordinary kindness on the part of the Blessed Virgin Mary towards the Russian population.' Mother Teresa was also struck by this and in her heart grew the great desire to work towards the conversion of Russia. From that moment on, she dedicated herself to this project with all her heart. [15]

Mother Teresa's loving heart was expanding even more as she prayed to help in some way with the requests of Our Lady, particularly with those expressed through the apparitions at Fatima. Bishop Hnilica helped Mother Teresa to get Miraculous Medals into communist countries:

> Mother Teresa was one of the greatest promoters of this medal. She always kept copies on her, which she handed out to whoever asked her for prayers. She recommended wearing it around the neck or in a pocket as a sign of protection…she saw that many of these medals arrived in Russia. She made me buy bags of them, and then I had them blessed by John Paul II, and we sent them clandestinely to Communist countries.

In 1984, Mother Teresa came up with a fascinating idea. She told her bishop friend that a Miraculous Medal had to be brought into the Kremlin "as if to consecrate the capital of atheism to the Virgin Mary with this simple gesture." Mother Teresa wanted to know if he could possibly carry out her project, a potential mission impossible in what is one of the most elite undercover espionage hubs in the world.

"To be honest, I was the least suitable person to do such a thing, because in the countries behind the Iron Curtain I was considered

Enemy Number One of Communism, and in Czechoslovakia, I had been condemned to death because of my anti-Communist activity. Entering into the Soviet Union was impossible for me, but I couldn't say no to Mother Teresa. Being with her, it was easy to get infected by her enthusiasm and courage," the Slovakian bishop recalled.

"I thus accepted to take the 'risk,' but I didn't know whether I'd succeed in completing the task." Mother Teresa had some contacts within the Russian Consulate in Calcutta. "I don't know what she said to them, but she managed to get me a visa," Bishop Hnilica said.

Knowing that on March 25, 1984, the Feast of the Annunciation, Pope John Paul II was going to consecrate Russia to the Immaculate Heart of Mary, Mother Teresa chose that date for this deeply undercover holy mission. "She wanted someone to be inside the Kremlin at the precise moment when the Pope recited the prayer of consecration in Rome, in order to pray spiritually with the Pope and leave one of the famous Miraculous Medals there," Bishop Hnilica recounted.

In mid-February 1984, Bishop Hnilica departed for Calcutta with a trusted traveling companion Msgr. Leo Maasburg. Certain of the importance of backing up important works with prayer, Mother Teresa prayerfully prepared for the journey. "For a whole month, we prayed together that our plans would work. Mother Teresa also made her nuns pray for 'a particular intention,' as apart from us two and Fr. Leo, no one else knew what we were about to do," said the bishop.

Mother Teresa, having arranged for the visa and flights through the Russian Consulate, set it up so that Bishop Hnilica and Fr. Leo would be tourists traveling from Calcutta to Rome via Moscow. The pit stop to Moscow would be for three days to visit the city's museums.

Mother Teresa accompanied the two of them to the Calcutta airport on March 23, 1984. "When I said goodbye to her, she was moved; she grasped my hand and gave me her personal rosary." Bishop Hnilica recalled.

The two "secret agents" arrived safely in Moscow without any problem, but a time of extreme panic for Bishop Hnilica was just around the corner. "I showed my passport to a soldier at the customs desk. He looked at me suspiciously, and then he began asking me a lot of questions." Bishop Hnilica explained that he didn't want the soldier to know that he spoke Russian so he answered in Italian. The soldier didn't seem to understand him and began to make phone calls from the guard room. Maybe since it was only five o'clock in the morning, no one answered on the other end.

"I had to wait outside the customs office where it was -5°C. I was worried, so I pulled out Mother Teresa's rosary from my pocket and secretly started to pray. I could already see myself deported to Siberia. But I also had a lot of faith in Mother Teresa's prayers. The nun had said that my journey would be accompanied by her constant prayers. I thus said: 'Lord, let your will be done! But remember that it is Mother Teresa who has sent me here.'"

After waiting for nearly an hour, Bishop Hnilica was called back inside. "I could see he was annoyed because he hadn't been able to contact any of his superiors. He tried yet again to ask me whether my passport was mine, and I nodded. In the end, he stamped my passport and let me go."

Finally, Bishop Hnilica joined Fr. Leo, his traveling companion and partner in Mother Teresa's plot, who had been waiting in a corner of the airport. After checking into their hotel, they began touring the area separately. The Kremlin just happened to be open for a few days for tourists, and Mother Teresa's two "secret agents" found out how to enter.

"The Kremlin is a citadel, surrounded by a wall within the city of Moscow. It is a type of fortress which extends over an area of twenty-eight hectares," the bishop explained. "In ancient times, it was the civil and religious heart of the city. There were, in fact, royal palaces and some of Moscow's most important churches, among which [is] the Orthodox Patriarchs' cathedral, called the [Cathedral] of the Dormition or Assumption Cathedral. After the Bolshevik revolution in 1918, these churches were closed and transformed into museums."

Mother Teresa had it carefully planned out. She asked Bishop Hnilica to visit the Kremlin on the morning of March 25 when Pope John Paul II was to begin his ceremony for the consecration of Russia to the Immaculate Heart of Mary. She specifically asked the bishop to pause in the Assumption Cathedral. He was to look as if he was a tourist admiring the art work. Mother Teresa asked him to pray while there and find the perfect spot to place the Miraculous Medal that she had given him.

Bishop Hnilica felt a bit frightened, but trusted that Mother Teresa was praying for this special mission. The Kremlin was filled with tourists that day, which helped to make the bishop feel more protected.

"I visited several buildings and stopped in the Archangel Cathedral, the second largest in the Kremlin. I then entered the Assumption Cathedral," he said. Bishop Hnilica carefully looked around the beautiful church (actually a museum now), rich in breathtaking works of art "to find a spot where I could deposit the medal," he recalled.

"I noticed, reading my guidebook, that there were the thrones where the tsar, tsarina, and Patriarch of Moscow and all Russia used to sit during the religious ceremonies, with the patriarch sitting in the middle. I decided that the Miraculous Medal should be put under the throne of the patriarch while praying that Patriarch Alexy

II would soon be able to return to celebrate religious rites in that place."

Bishop Hnilica decided to carry out a secret Mass while he was there. He used a piece of bread and some wine that he had brought with him and carried out the consecration from memory. "This was an intensely moving and religious moment. A Mass had not been celebrated in this place for seventy-six years," he pointed out. "Then, very slowly, I approached the patriarch's throne, and I noticed a little crack in the wooden floor where I quickly dropped the Miraculous Medal. I remained there for a while longer praying, and then I went back to the hotel where Fr. Leo was waiting for me. We left for Italy on the same afternoon."

A few months later Bishop Hnilica gave a detailed account to Mother Teresa when she visited Rome. She was very happy to know that the sacramental of the blessed Miraculous Medal was in place at the time of the consecration. Mother Teresa continued in her missionary work on behalf of Russia.

One day in 1988, Mother Teresa called Bishop Hnilica to let him know that she had been invited to Moscow for an international meeting and was on her way to the airport.

She met Raisa Gorbachev, the wife of the secretary general of the Soviet Union. They became friends, and Mother Teresa confided to Mrs. Gorbachev her wish to open a few convents for nuns in Russia. Mrs. Gorbachev promised to help. The first convent opened just one year later.

Mother Teresa had expressed her wish to Bishop Hnilica. "My dream is to be able to open fifteen convents in Russia, because there are fifteen mysteries in the rosary." Instead, even more convents were opened. Twenty to be exact. Interestingly, there are the same number of convents in the Soviet Union as there are mysteries in the rosary because Pope John Paul II has since added five more mysteries to the traditional fifteen mysteries of the rosary. Mother Teresa's dream came true.[16]

A Time to Reflect

Do you have a "dwelling place" of the Blessed Mother where you can pray and reflect? St. John Paul II said that a dwelling place for Mother Mary can be "a special corner in the home or little wayside shrines adorned with an image of the Mother of God, to chapels and churches built in her honor."[17] Wherever it is, place yourself near Mary's Immaculate Heart while you are in prayer. Confide to her all of your interests and desires. Ask her to grant her graces to you and bring you closer to her Son Jesus.

If you have not done so already, you might want to consider creating a special place in your home in which to keep company with the Mother of God. It might be accomplished by simply adding a statue or image of Mary to a corner of your home. Or, you might do something more elaborate. You can find more information about how to consecrate your family to the Immaculate Heart in Appendix A.

In My Own Life

Do you take time to think about the Blessed Mother? Life is busy. But can you carve a bit more time to learn more about her and also ponder her life? Reading this book gives the history of Our Lady of Fatima and her peace plan.

When you are in need of peace in your own life, do you pray to the Blessed Mother, seeking her intercession? One time when I was on complete bed rest during a precarious pregnancy in which my doctor told me I was losing my baby, Mother Teresa sent me a Miraculous Medal and offered some simple yet powerful prayers to me. I had lost three babies to miscarriage before that pregnancy, and the doctors had warned us that the outcome to this particular pregnancy was not looking very promising. I had to keep still and keep praying for God's holy will—whatever that would be. I was put in a position in which I needed to totally trust God.

One of the prayers that Mother Teresa sent to me during this difficult time has stayed with me: "Mary, Mother of Jesus, be Mother to me now." We certainly need Mary now. I prayed that prayer quite a bit and did my best to trust God…and my daughter Mary-Catherine was born after a long nine months of staying still to preserve her life. She is twenty-five years old today as I write this book!

In what area of your life is God asking you to trust him now? Ask Mary to be Mother to you and lead you closer to the heart of her Son!

PRAYER

Mary, Mother of Jesus, be Mother to me now!

Chapter Two

THE ANGEL OF PEACE APPARITIONS

Do not be afraid. I am the Angel of Peace.

—angel appearing to the children at Fatima

Let's step back now to the spring of 1916, when God sent the Angel of Peace three times to prepare the future visionaries of Fatima. The three young shepherds were out at one of their usual grazing spots, called the Cabeco, tending their families' sheep, and unexpectedly encountered a mysterious heavenly visitor for the first time. Nine-year-old Lucia dos Santos and her younger cousins Francisco, eight, and Jacinto Marto, six, were a tight-knit trio who delighted in the familiar routines of their childhood: caring for their family's sheep, praying the rosary together after lunch, and playing games.

Though they were young, they knew how important it was to keep an eye on the flock. In her *Memoirs*, the oldest, Lucia, described the importance of the flocks and the duty of watching over them. She said:

> As soon as the children reached the age of seven, they began to take their share in the running of the house by being taught how to look after the flocks. Like the Patriarchs and Kings of old, nearly every family had its little flock of gentle sheep which the children led out to graze in the green fields belonging to the parents. The flock helped considerably towards the maintenance of the family: milk and cheese, lambs to replace sheep that have grown old, or for sale on the market; wool which women of the house used to spin, dye, and then weave, in order to use later, to

make warm colored shawls for the winter, or to make mats for the humble bedrooms, or round blue serge skirts with red stripes to adorn the Sunday clothes worn by the girls."[1]

It was during one of these normal, quiet days in 1916 that the Lord sent his Angel of Peace to prepare the children for what was to come. Before we get into the heavenly visits from the Angel of Peace, it's important to note that in 1915, only one year earlier, Lucia encountered mysterious manifestations when she was on the top of Monte do Cabeço with three companions: Teresa Matias, her sister Maria Rose, and Maria Justino. She tells about it in her *Memoirs*:

> We had hardly begun when, there before our eyes, we saw a figure poised in the air above the trees; it looked like a statue made of snow, rendered almost transparent by the rays of the sun.
>
> "What is that?" asked my companions, quite frightened.
>
> "I don't know!"
>
> We went on praying, with our eyes fixed on the figure before us, and as we finished our prayer, the figure disappeared."[2]

The First Angel Apparition

One day, after the three children had eaten lunch and quickly prayed their rosary—for they were eager to get started on their games—a strong gust of wind instantly grabbed their attention. The nearby treetops began to shake with great force, and suddenly a radiant white angel appeared. He looked to be a young man.

The cousins could not believe their eyes. Lucia described her observation of the encounter with the celestial being as "[a] young man, about fourteen or fifteen years old, whiter than snow, transparent as crystal when the sun shines through it and of great beauty."[3]

The angel had come to the children bearing a strong reassurance, as well as an awe-inspiring invitation to prayer.

"Do not be afraid. I am the Angel of Peace. Pray with me."[4]

Angels are found in both the Old and New Testaments. Their very existence invites us to pray with them, to praise and glorify God. Hebrews 1:14 says, "Are not all angels spirits in the divine service, sent to serve for the sake of those who are to inherit salvation?" Angels behold the face of God and at the same time help us. They work continuously on our behalf transporting our prayers to God and always guiding us to be good and pleasing to God. We need to make a point to be attentive to the inspiration of our guardian angels.

Lucia, Francisco, and Jacinta could never have imagined a visit from heaven! It was the farthest thing from their minds as they were grazing their sheep in the Cabeco that spring day. But immediately after seeing the startling appearance of brilliant white radiance from their visitor, the subsequent words and gestures from the Angel of Peace put the children at ease. Still, they didn't react in any way other than to follow the angel's instructions. They did not consult with one another. They were so deeply touched by the heavenly visitor.

The angel's posture expressed a deep reverence. He knelt and bowed, touching his forehead to the ground. When he remained in that position, the children felt called to imitate the holy messenger. Unlike Lucia and Jacinta, Francisco could not hear the angel speak. But he could certainly see him and followed the gestures precisely and also his sister's and cousin's words and actions. Lucia recalled, "Led by a supernatural impulse, we did the same, and repeated the words which we heard him say."[5] The angel then proceeded to teach the children a special prayer that they had never heard before. This prayer is now referred to as the Pardon Prayer.

> My God, I believe, I adore, I hope, and I love You! I beg pardon
> for those who do not believe, do not adore, do not hope, and do
> not love You.

The Angel of Peace repeated this prayer three times. Then he rose and, looking at the children, said, "Pray thus. The hearts of Jesus and Mary are attentive to the voice of your supplications."

Then as suddenly as he had appeared, the angel vanished.

What were the young visionaries to think of this? Well, truth be told, they did not think of anything but to remain kneeling in prayer for quite some time. The apparition had certainly made an extraordinary impact on their hearts and souls. God's love permeated their beings, and they were being transformed.

Lucia later recalled the intense supernatural atmosphere that influenced them. They felt the presence of God carry over with them into the following day, during which time they remained speechless. They understood that something miraculous had happened, but they could not imagine that the Most High God was predisposing them to later receive his plan of mercy. Unbeknownst to them they were being prepared for something even more astonishing than what they had just experienced.

The words of the prayer given to the young visionaries may seem simple. But the words outline our responsibilities as Christians—to believe, to adore, to hope, and to love God. As well, to ask pardon for those who do not act in this way. And further, to beg pardon for them. We should make reparation for their sins too.

In teaching this prayer, the angel introduced the children to intercessory prayer for sinners. We too can pray this prayer sincerely, and we can endeavor to make reparation for sinners. We, like the children, can learn from the Angel of Peace and strive to be more reverent in saying our prayers.

The occurrence of the visit from the Angel of Peace was at a time when many people were losing their faith and World War I was causing much sorrow and suffering. Just as it was important to pray and ask pardon for sinners in Lucia, Francisco, and Jacinta's time, it is important in our modern time as well. I might go so far as to say that the prayer very well may be even more important now.

Fr. Andrew Apostoli, CFR, author of *Fatima for Today* said, "When we pray the Pardon Prayer we are praying for faith, hope and charity to be renewed in the world.... By praying for those who are not praying for themselves, we can hope that God will grant to those souls the graces to begin praying on their own. We can trust Jesus and Mary will always be attentive to this prayer!"[6]

The Second Angel Apparition

Sometime during the summer of that same year, the Angel of Peace visited the cousins again. The children did not keep a record of dates and times. It wasn't customary to keep track of time. But the young shepherds were familiar with the seasons.

Once again, the angel appeared during a normal day. As the children were playing, the Angel of Peace was suddenly beside them.

"What are you doing?" he asked. The angel did not wait for an answer, but instead gave them a direct, loving command.

"Pray! Pray very much! The hearts of Jesus and Mary have designs of mercy on you. Offer prayers and sacrifices constantly to the Most High."[7]

Lucia, Francisco, and Jacinta took the angel's words to heart. They began to pray more than they had ever prayed before, knowing that Jesus and Mary were depending on them to help with their prayers. They began to pray the Pardon Prayer frequently. The children might have been more mindful of prayer than most children their age, but they were now being instructed to use their time more wisely by offering up sacrifices and prayers to God for sinners. In fact, the angel used the word "constantly." Jesus and Mary were counting on them. What a huge responsibility!

Because Jesus and Mary had "designs of mercy" on Lucia, Francisco, and Jacinta, it was essential for the children to step up their prayer lives and be open to God's graces for them. Lucia asked the angel how they should make the sacrifices. She immediately received her answer. The angel said:

> Make of everything you can a sacrifice, and offer it to God as an act of reparation for the sins by which He is offended, and in supplication for the conversion of sinners. You will thus draw down peace upon your country. I am its Angel Guardian, the Angel of Portugal. Above all, accept and bear with submission, the suffering which the Lord will send you.[8]

The angel then disappeared. Again, Francisco learned what the angel said from the girls because he did not hear the angel speaking. The children now knew that the Angel of Peace was also the guardian angel of Portugal.

They had much to ponder about their new role in making sacrifices to help convert sinners and make up for the sins that deeply offended God. The young shepherds were learning that their prayers, actions, and attitudes could even aid their country, by God's graces to bring peace. It was a lot for them to take in, but they believed the Angel of Peace and wanted to please God. Imagine being spiritually trained by an angel!

The children were deeply enlightened by the angel's visit. Lucia would sum it up later on in her *Memoirs:*

> These words were indelibly impressed upon our minds. They were like a light which made us understand who God is, how He loves us and desires to be loved, the value of sacrifice, how pleasing it is to Him, and how, on account of it, He grants the grace of conversion to sinners.[9]

The Third Angel Apparition

In the fall of 1916, in the month of September or October, the children were out in the Cabeco grazing their sheep when the angel visited for the third time. This was the same place that the angel had appeared during the first apparition. Several months had passed since the angel's second apparition, in which he lovingly rebuked them for not praying enough.

The children had been faithful to their prayers and praying the Pardon Prayer, as the angel had taught them. In fact, they were kneeling with their heads bowed, touching the ground, while their flock grazed nearby when, without warning, a bright light illuminated their surroundings and shown brilliantly upon them.

A bit startled, the little shepherds lifted their heads and discovered the Angel of Peace was back again. In fact, he was right next to them, holding a chalice in his left hand. A Eucharistic Host was hovering over the chalice, and distinctly defined drops of Jesus's Precious Blood were falling from the Sacred Host into the chalice.

The angel left the chalice and Host suspended in the air to kneel down beside Lucia, Francisco, and Jacinta. They were being called to Adoration. Reverently, they bowed down with the angel, lowering their foreheads to touch the ground in Adoration before Jesus in the Blessed Sacrament.

The angel taught Lucia, Francisco, and Jacinta another important prayer:

> Most Holy Trinity, Father, Son, and Holy Spirit, I adore You profoundly, and I offer You the most Precious Body, Blood, Soul and Divinity of Jesus Christ, present in all the tabernacles of the world, in reparation for the outrages, sacrileges and indifference with which He Himself is offended. And through the infinite merits of His Most Sacred Heart, and the Immaculate Heart of Mary, I beg of you the conversion of poor sinners.[10]

The Angel of Peace told them to repeat the prayer three times. After this, the angel rose and took the chalice and Host into his hands. He approached Lucia and gave her the Host. He then gave Jacinta and Francisco the chalice.

"Take and drink the Body and Blood of Jesus Christ, horribly outraged by ungrateful men. Repair their crimes and console your God."[11]

Lucia was the only one of the three to have already made her First Holy Communion. The drinking from the chalice that day was Francisco's and Jacinta's First Holy Communion!

Again the Angel of Peace bowed down to the ground and thrice prayed the prayer which he had just taught them. The reverent actions of the angel and God's mysterious graces beckoned the young shepherds to do the same.

When the angel disappeared, the children remained in prayer. Even at their tender age, they committed to offer their lives completely to God through the Eucharistic sacrifice they had just received. God's grace was working powerfully in their hearts as they were being prepared to meet the Queen of Heaven!

A TIME TO REFLECT

The Angel of Peace and, later on, the Blessed Mother would teach the children that there are outrages, sacrileges, and indifferences which offend Jesus in the Eucharist. Prayers and acts of reparation could help to repair the damages and even convert sinners. Fr. Andrew Apostoli, CFR, gives examples of outrages, sacrileges, and indifference.

Fr. Apostoli said, "Desecration of the Eucharist is an outrage. Knowingly receiving Holy Communion in mortal sin would be a sacrilege. Indifference would include talking in church or receiving Holy Communion without adequate preparation." What can we do?

"We have to make reparation for these offenses. The Eucharist occupies a very important place in the message of Fatima, which we must respond to."

Fr. Apostoli added, "St. John Bosco foresaw that some of the greatest trials in the Church's history would occur in the 20th century and that only by devotion to the Eucharist and to the Immaculate Heart of Mary would the Church be saved."[12]

The Angel of Peace appeared three times to Lucia, Francisco, and Jacinta to prepare them for the great message of Our Lady of Fatima. The angel showed a profound reverence for Jesus in the Holy Eucharist when he appeared to the shepherd children. What can you learn from the Angel of Peace?

We each have our own guardian angel gifted to us by God as a perfect and steadfast guide, as well as a holy companion. Do we remember our angel's presence every day? Do we call upon him for help, asking him to teach us how to grow in holiness?

St. John Vianney taught that we should imitate the angels in their consciousness of the presence of God. In his "Sermon on Holy Communion," he said, "We ought to ask the Blessed Virgin, the angels, and the saints to pray for us that we may receive the good God as worthily as it is possible for us to receive Him."[13]

Ponder these words and pray that your own guardian angel will enlighten you and guide you on the path to heaven. Here is a simple prayer:

Angel of God, my guardian dear, to whom God's love commits me here. Ever this day be at my side, to light and guard, to rule and guide. Amen.

IN MY OWN LIFE

In light of the Angel of Peace apparitions in which the angel's visits were meant to prepare the children's hearts, do you recall a time in your own spiritual journey when God might have been preparing you for something greater? Granted, we do not all receive the awesome privilege of visits by angels! As well, we are not all called to such great missions as the children. Yet, each one of us has the responsibility to grow in holiness and to strive to help one another get to heaven. St. Teresa of Calcutta, whom I was blessed to know personally, would say often, "Holiness is not the luxury of a few, but a simple duty for you and me."[14]

How can you become more attentive to God and more faithful to prayer? Can you ponder a possible plan and put it into practice soon? Hopefully, you can incorporate the prayers taught by the Angel of Peace into your daily life.

PRAYER

Dear Lord Jesus, help me to be more attentive to you in my life. Forgive me for the times I have neglected to listen to you speaking to my heart. Help me to make a more concerted effort to be prayerful. Please help me to be mindful about my responsibility in leading others to you and away from sin. Thank you for the gift of my guardian angel whom I desire to pray to more often.

Blessed Mother Mary, Our Lady of Fatima, please guide me closer to your Son Jesus. All of the angels and saints, please help me to be strong against the evil influences in this world by avoiding temptation, by praying constantly, and by leading a virtuous life. Amen.

Pardon Prayer (taught by the Angel of Peace): My God, I believe, I adore, I hope, and I love You! I beg pardon for those who do not believe, do not adore, do not hope, and do not love You. *(Pray three times.)*

Most Holy Trinity Prayer (taught by the Angel of Peace): Most Holy Trinity, Father, Son, and Holy Spirit, I adore You profoundly, and I offer You the most Precious Body, Blood, Soul, and Divinity of Jesus

Christ, present in all the tabernacles of the world, in reparation for the outrages, sacrileges, and indifference with which He Himself is offended. And through the infinite merits of His Most Sacred Heart, and the Immaculate Heart of Mary, I beg of you the conversion of poor sinners. *(Pray three times.)*

Chapter Three

THE FIRST TWO APPARITIONS OF OUR LADY OF FATIMA

Do not be afraid. I will do you no harm.
—first words of Our Lady of Fatima to the shepherd children

What Are the Apparitions of Our Lady of Fatima?

In a document entitled *The Message of Fatima*, the Congregation for the Doctrine of the Faith declared that "Fatima is undoubtedly the most prophetic of modern apparitions." To understand the reason for this, we should look first at the historical context in which these messages were revealed.

Though the Angel of Peace had visited three times—and the children were undoubtedly changed by these visits—the reality of World War I was still a terrible one for the Portuguese people in early 1917. In the midst of the spiritual, physical, and emotional agony of the war, Pope Benedict XV called for a novena to be said to Our Lady, the Queen of Peace.

May 13, 1917, was the eighth day of the novena.

On that spring day, Lucia, Francisco, and Jacinta were once again with their flocks in the Cova da Iria. It had been roughly eight months since they'd been visited by the Angel of Peace.

The First Apparition: May 13, 1917

After getting the flocks out to the pasture on that stunningly sunny day, the children sat down on the ground to eat their simple lunches. As always, they said their prayers and hurried through the rosary. The sheep were content pulling at the blades of grass, and the children were eager to play their games.

Suddenly, what seemed like a bolt of lightning dazzled the sky with brilliant light. The startled children rushed to round up their flocks, as storms were dangerous in the open fields. But before they could get to their sheep, another flash summoned their attention. They stood in amazement before a beautiful Lady dressed in white, who was positioned on a holm oak tree. Lucia described the scene in her *Memoirs*: "She seemed more brilliant than the sun, and radiated light more clear and intense than a crystal glass filled with sparkling water, when the rays of the burning sun shine through it."[1] The beautiful Lady immediately put the children at ease. She said, "Do not be afraid. I will do you no harm."[2]

Lucia wrote, "I think that these words of Our Lady—*Do not be afraid*—did not refer to any actual fear we might have had of Her, because She knew well we were not frightened of Her. The words must have referred to the fear that had caused us to hurry away from the supposed thunderstorm in which we thought we were going to get caught."[3]

Imagine the surprise, as well as delight and curiosity, the children felt when the peaceful, mysterious Lady spoke to them! The Lady had a young, glowing countenance. In fact, Lucia later said that she looked to be about seventeen years old, wearing a mantle and a tunic that seemed to be made of light. A cord with a little ball of light hung from her neck and towards the bottom of her tunic was a star. The Lady was holding rosary beads, which were as brilliant as stars—the crucifix seeming to give off the most radiant light of all.

The previous year the Angel of Peace had also put the children at ease when he told them to not be afraid. Now they were in the presence of a mysterious, beautiful Lady who greeted them with the same message. Francisco and Jacinta watched and listened attentively, though Francisco could not hear the Lady's voice.

Lucia spoke up. "Where are you from?"

"I am from heaven," the beautiful Lady answered.

Lucia did not hesitate to ask the next question: "What do you want of me?"

The Lady replied, "I have come to ask you to come here for six months in succession, on the thirteenth day, at this same hour. Later on, I will tell you who I am and what I want. Afterwards, I will return here yet a seventh time."

Lucia had another question pressing on her heart. "Shall I go to heaven too?"

The Lady answered, "Yes, you will."

Lucia asked, "And Jacinta?"

"She will go also," the Lady said.

"And Francisco?" Lucia wanted to know.

"He will go there too, but he must say many rosaries," the Lady explained.[4]

Many years later, Lucia wrote, "I think that this special injunction to Francisco is for all of us. It is not that saying many rosaries, as such, is an indispensable condition for going to Heaven, but that we must pray much."[5]

Lucia was curious and also concerned about two friends who had recently died. She asked the Lady about her sixteen-year-old friend. "Is Maria Neves already in heaven?"

The beautiful Lady answered. "Yes, she is."

"And Amelia?" asked Lucia about her almost-twenty-year-old friend. Perhaps Lucia wasn't prepared for the Lady's answer.

"She will be in purgatory until the end of the world."

Reflecting upon that sobering answer, Lucia later wrote, "The reply Our Lady gave confirms that there is a Purgatory, and is at the same time yet another proof of the need we have to pray."[6]

Suffer and Pray

The beautiful Lady then asked the children if they would accept their heavenly mission. "Are you willing to offer yourselves to God and bear all the sufferings He wills to send you, as an act of reparation for the sins by which He is offended, and of supplication for the conversion of sinners?"

"Yes, we are willing," the children answered, enthusiastic in their heartfelt desire to save souls. The Angel of Peace had prepared their hearts for this special mission. Otherwise, the children might not have understood the depth of this great entrustment and might not have responded affirmatively so quickly and passionately.

"Then you are going to have much to suffer," the beautiful Lady warned. "But the grace of God will be your comfort," she reassured them.[7]

Though their hearts were prepared by the angel's apparitions, and now the comfort from the beautiful Lady, they still did not have any idea about how quickly their lives of suffering would unfold.

But before they could even try to fathom what was in store for them, a transforming, radiant light enveloped them and pierced their hearts, bringing comfort to their souls. The holy light came forth from the blessed Lady's hands. Lucia later described the experience. She wrote:

> Our Lady opened both her hands for the first time, communicating to us a light so intense that, as it streamed from her hands, its rays penetrated our hearts and the innermost depths of our souls, making us see ourselves in God, Who was that light, more clearly than we see ourselves in the best of mirrors. Then, moved by an interior impulse that was also communicated to us, we fell on our knees, repeating in our hearts:
>
> "O most Holy Trinity, I adore you! My God, my God, I love You in the most Blessed Sacrament!"[8]

The shepherd children repeated the prayer and remained kneeling in the transforming heavenly light. The beautiful Lady would soon leave them. Before doing so, she requested from them another important commitment. "Pray the rosary every day to obtain peace in the world, and an end of the war."[9]

The three visionaries were entrusted with two great heavenly responsibilities on that day. They were to begin offering sufferings and sacrifices for the benefit of sinners. As well, they were to pray the rosary daily to obtain peace in the world and even to end World War I. Could children really help to end a war? With heaven's powerful rosary, peace could be obtained, according to the beautiful Lady.

The beautiful Lady departed from their company as heaven seemed to open for her and she disappeared from their sight.

Keeping Secrets

Suffering, indeed, came to the children, unfolding in a way that they were not expecting—through the ones that loved them. Lucia had instinctively asked Francisco and Jacinta to keep the visions a secret. The Lady had not asked that of them, but Lucia sensed that it was best to keep it all quiet. Despite her warnings and her younger cousins' promises, their secret was soon revealed.

Little Jacinta could not contain her excitement over what had happened. She waited by the gate for her mother to come home that day. Her mother and father had gone out to buy a pig. Upon seeing her mother, Jacinta hugged her tightly and then told her everything, right there at the gate. Her mother, Olimpia, thought her daughter's imagination was galloping away uncontrollably, like a runaway horse.

After mulling it over, her father, Ti Marto, came to believe his daughter's story. Jacinta's brother Francisco had maintained the exact same story, and he had never lied before. In addition, thinking that the beautiful Lady must have been the Virgin Mary, Ti Marto believed that since the Blessed Mother had appeared in other places, it very well could be her appearing to his children. At least there was someone in the children's corner. Their siblings laughed and poked fun at them.

Meanwhile, Lucia's mother, Maria Rosa, was very angry with her daughter when she got wind of the alleged sightings. She was not taking any of it lightly, believing Lucia to be responsible for committing a serious sin and even of being blasphemous. The family had already experienced some troubling difficulties. Maria Rosa feared even worse repercussions. Poor Lucia was mocked by her own family, as well as her neighbors and some friends. In later years she revealed that her mother's and sister's contentious attitude cut her to the heart. She said it was "indeed as hurtful to me as insults."[10]

Young Jacinta felt terrible about making things tough for Lucia. She apologized to Lucia, who immediately forgave her. Jacinta also deeply reflected on the Lady's visit. She felt bad about rushing through her earlier rosaries and vowed to pray her future rosaries with love and devotion.

The three of them talked about this amongst themselves. Francisco came up with the idea to feed their lunches to the sheep in order to make sacrifices to convert sinners. They later decided to give their food to any people in need that they would see when bringing their sheep out to the pastures. They also decided to deprive themselves of drinking water, even on the boiling hot summer days out in the dry, rocky fields, as a sacrifice to help the Lady. This was all done in secret.

Meanwhile, Maria Rosa was determined to convince her parish priest to put pressure on Lucia so that she would recant her crazy story. She wanted the whole thing nipped in the bud before it grew worse and embarrassed the family even further. Fr. Manuel Ferreira met with Lucia and listened to her story. The interrogations made

Lucia feel uncomfortable, but the young visionary told the truth about what she had seen and heard.

Fr. Ferreira then gave Lucia's mother some prudent advice. He urged her to wait and see what would unfold in time. He counseled Lucia's mother to allow her to go to the Cova. Maria Rosa was not very happy about Fr. Ferreira's findings, but she chose to heed his advice.

All of this kind of heartache, suffering, and scrutiny went on for Lucia throughout the remainder of the time before the beautiful Lady was going to be coming back as she had promised. The ridicule and heartache Lucia suffered made her feel utterly worn out. The beautiful encounter with the Lady seemed to vanish as quickly in her mind as when the Lady herself had disappeared into heaven. And now, Lucia was left with three things weighing on her—a promise from the Lady that she would return; her own promises to the Lady of her willingness to suffer, offer, and pray the rosary; and an almost unbearable suffering in not being believed by those she loved.

This third burden was the heaviest for Lucia. It weighed upon her spirit so that Lucia began to wonder if she should even go back to the Cova. Deep plaguing doubts caused her to wonder if the devil could be behind the Lady's appearance like some said.

Little Francisco and Jacinta continued to encourage Lucia. June 13 approached, and Lucia's doubts faded as the urge to go to see the heavenly Lady overtook her heart and soul. When the morning came, she ran to Francisco and Jacinta's house to tell them that she would go.

The Second Apparition: June 13, 1917

Ever since the beautiful Lady had appeared above the holm oak tree, word had spread throughout the village of Fatima and surrounding areas. Many people mocked the children for their story of the alleged encounter with a heavenly visitor. But there were also those who wished to believe.

One month later, on June 13, many townspeople gathered to pray the rosary near the tree. In accordance to the Lady's promise, they anticipated a heavenly visit from the Lady from heaven as she had promised the children that she would come back on this date. First, the people attended the church celebration that morning to St. Anthony (1195—1231), a great patron of Portugal, at the parish church named after him.

Lucia's mother hoped that her daughter would choose to attend the daylong feast day festivities for St. Anthony of Padua rather than go to the Cova that day. Lucia's sister Maria dos Anjos later recalled, "Our mother knew well how Lucia loved the festa, and she hoped the whole story of the Cova da Iria would pass with it." The day prior, their mother had said, "It is a good thing that we are having St. Anthony tomorrow...and we mustn't say anything to Lucia about going to the Cova. We must talk of nothing but the festa so that by tomorrow she will have forgotten the other foolishness."[11]

But Lucia was not going to miss seeing the Lady. That morning she couldn't finish her bread and cheese breakfast fast enough. The three young shepherds dressed up in their Sunday best. Some parishioners followed them to the Cova da Iria, where they came upon the others already there waiting.

As noon approached, the children knelt down to pray the rosary. The others knelt too and prayed along with them. When they finished the rosary, the three young shepherds saw the heavenly light again. It was coming towards them. Then the special Lady was right there on the holm oak tree as she had been the last time.

Again Lucia asked the question burning in her heart, "What do you want of me?"

"I wish you to come here on the thirteenth of next month, to pray the rosary every day, and to learn to read. Later, I will tell you what I want," the Lady replied.

The Lady's requests were simple and direct. But this was the first time that she asked Lucia to learn to read. Reading would become an important part of Lucia's mission in spreading the messages of Our Lady of Fatima.

Lucia asked the beautiful Lady if she would cure a sick person that she knew. The Lady answered, "If he is converted, he will be cured during the year." (We don't have any other details about this person. But we can gather that in order to receive cures or favors from heaven we must be properly disposed. We must believe and have faith.)

Next Lucia wanted to ask about heaven again. The Lady had told her at the first visit that all three cousins would go to heaven. Lucia was bold. She asked, "I would like to ask you to take us to heaven."

"Yes. I will take Jacinta and Francisco soon. But you are to stay here some time longer. Jesus wishes to make use of you to make me known and loved. He wants to establish in the world devotion to my Immaculate Heart," the Lady replied.

We can imagine the joy experienced by Jacinta and Francisco knowing that they would be privileged to go to heaven soon. And though Lucia had already been assured that she would also go to heaven, she was now told that she had to wait for "some time." It was bittersweet to know she had a mission when she also longed for heaven along with her younger cousins.

"Am I to stay here alone?" Lucia asked.

The Lady's answer was warm and reassuring. She said, "No, my daughter. Are you suffering a great deal? Don't lose heart. I will never forsake you. My Immaculate Heart will be your refuge and the way that will lead you to God."[12]

Suddenly the Lady opened her hands like she had at the apparition in May. Immediately, a heavenly light was bestowed upon the three children, wrapping them in great brilliance. Lucia later recalled, "In front of the palm of Our Lady's right hand was a heart encircled by thorns which pierced it. We understood that this was the Immaculate Heart of Mary, outraged by the sins of humanity, and seeking reparation."[13]

The children were eager to make up for those sins and outrages committed against the Immaculate Heart of Mary. Through the graces that the Lady was bestowing upon them, they came to love the Immaculate Heart in a profound way.

In the heavenly light, the children were mysteriously submerged in God. Jacinta and Francisco could be seen as in a light rising to heaven and Lucia was in light spreading over the earth. This vision of light enveloping the children was consistent with what the Lady said about their future with regard to heaven.

The beautiful Lady then faded away into heaven.

A Time to Reflect

The Blessed Mother entrusted a great mission to three children. They could have run away from the vision and from the Lady speaking to them. They could have listened and watched, then ignored the whole thing. But they chose to believe and take it to their hearts.

The children were asked if they would offer sufferings and sacrifices to save souls. Even in such tender years, they agreed! They cared. They desired to help others and didn't worry that they wouldn't be strong enough to carry out what was asked of them. They trusted. Do we have the same love in our hearts? Could our hearts be hardened from life's experiences or by sin? Take some time to sit still, unplug from technology, and think about what God might be calling you to do.

In My Own Life

Was there a time in your life when you turned your back on God? If so, have you asked forgiveness? Can you let go of the past and move forward in God's love? Can you trust God with your life?

The Blessed Mother told the children that they would receive all of the graces they needed to follow God's holy will in their lives. There is nothing to worry about when we trust God.

Prayer

Dear Lord Jesus, please open my heart to your love for me. Help me to trust you. Help me to let go of sins in the past and move forward in your love. Blessed Mother Mary, please pray for me and grant me the graces that I need. St. Joseph, guide me, please. All of the angels and saints, please pray for me. Amen.

Chapter Four

THE THREE SECRETS OF FATIMA REVEALED

Sacrifice yourselves for sinners, and say many times, especially whenever you make some sacrifice: O Jesus, it is for love of You, for the conversion of sinners, and in reparation for the sins committed against the Immaculate Heart of Mary.[1]

Receiving the Secrets of Fatima

In the month following the second visit, Lucia was tormented with doubts. She said these doubts disappeared completely on July 13, 1917. When Our Lady appeared on that day, she revealed to the children what are known as the "three secrets of Fatima."

The secrets have inspired many questions over the years. What exactly were they, and why were they considered *secrets* in the first place? What is the mystery behind the Third Secret of Fatima, and why was this prophetic vision veiled by the Vatican until the year 2000? Is there a controversy over the secrets? We will explore all of this.

The May and June apparitions were filled with mystery and excitement. The July apparition seemed to open a whole new dimension. Suddenly, the Lady's messages became even more serious than before. The children were still not exactly sure who she was, but they trusted her. The Lady spoke about the end of World War I, but warned about calamities, famines, persecutions, and a worse war to come if the people did not listen to her warnings and change their lives. She also told them about her Immaculate Heart, which had been revealed to them at the end of the June apparition when she opened her hands to heavenly light. An image of a heart surrounded by thorns appeared, symbolizing the outrages and sins committed against the Immaculate Heart of Mary.

Word had continued to get around Fatima and surrounding parts about the heavenly visitor who had appeared the last two months. People wanted to believe that it was the Blessed Mother that was visiting their area—perhaps to bestow special gifts on the people there. There were those, as well, who did not believe and wanted to cause a ruckus, or at least to see for themselves that it must be a clever trick from the devil.

Raymond Leo Cardinal Burke, archbishop emeritus of St. Louis and patron of the Sovereign Military Order of Malta wrote:

> The Blessed Virgin Mary came to visit mankind at Fatima at a time when many had grown forgetful of God and his all-loving plan for our salvation, and many had grown rebellious before the Law of God by which he orders all things for our good. Having alienated themselves from the universal love that comes to us from God alone, they fell prey to a destructive selfishness of heart, which was most dramatically and tragically manifested in the horror of the First World War. The great temptation in a world beset with the gravest evils was to lose hope in divine love and thus to cease responding to divine love with pure and selfless love. Knowing the severity of the temptation that his children were suffering, God the Father sent to earth the Blessed Virgin Mary, the mother of his only-begotten Son, in fidelity to her Mission as Mother of God, which she first accepted at the Annunciation and which she expressed so clearly at the Wedding Feast of Cana.[2]

During this July apparition, the Blessed Mother revealed a big "secret" in three parts to the children. These secrets are sometimes referred to as "three secrets" such as: the "First Secret," "Second Secret," and "Third Secret." Sometimes the secrets are referred to as one "secret" in three parts. However, for ease of reading, we will refer to them as three secrets rather than three parts of a one secret.

Lucia detailed the first two secrets in one of her *Memoirs* on August 31, 1941 (by that time she had long been professed as a Carmelite nun). On January 3, 1944, Sister Lucia wrote about the Third Secret in a separate manuscript by order of His Excellency, the Bishop of Leiria. The bishop kept the writings in a sealed envelope for a time. Sister Lucia wrote on the outside of the envelope that it could be opened only after 1960, either by the Patriarch of Lisbon or the Bishop of Leiria.

Sister Lucia recalls: "Archbishop Bertone therefore asked: 'Why only after 1960? Was it Our Lady who fixed that date?' Sister Lucia replied: 'It was not Our Lady. I fixed the date because I had the intuition that before 1960 it would not be understood, but that only later would it be understood.... I wrote down what I saw; however it was not for me to interpret it, but for the Pope.'"[3]

On April 4, 1957, the sealed envelope was transferred to a secret archive at the Vatican. Because of the great secrecy, curiosities were piqued and many rumors were spread about its contents. Pope John Paul II would finally reveal the Third Secret on May 13, 2000, at the beatification of Francisco and Jacinta Marto, which took place in the Cova da Iria.

The Third Apparition: July 13, 1917

On the morning of July 13, 1917, about four thousand people had gathered at the Cova da Iria in anticipation of the visit from the heavenly Lady. Many were praying the rosary before the Lady arrived. Suddenly, the heavenly light appeared as it had done previously, and the Lady was again over the holm oak tree.

Just as she had done before, Lucia spoke up with her usual question. "What do you want of me?"

The Lady answered as she had in the past but was now more explicit in her directions. "I want you to come here on the thirteenth of next month, to continue to pray the rosary every day in honor of Our Lady of the rosary, in order to obtain peace for the world and the end to the war, because only she can help you."

Young Lucia wanted the Lady to give her some more answers and to even prove herself to the crowds. "I would like to ask you to tell us who you are, and to work a miracle so that everybody will believe that you are appearing to us."

"Continue to come here every month," the Lady replied. "In October, I will tell you who I am and what I want, and I will perform a miracle for all to see and believe." She added, "Sacrifice yourselves for sinners, and say many times, especially whenever you make some sacrifice: O Jesus, it is for love of You, for the conversion of sinners, and in reparation for the sins committed against the Immaculate Heart of Mary."[4]

The Lady opened her hands as she was finishing the prayer, and rays of light came forth. But the light was not at all like the previous times. This time the light seemed to open the earth! The children immediately saw a great sea of fire and the most frightening scene unfold right before them. The First Secret of Fatima was a vision of hell. Lucia later described it:

> The rays of light seemed to penetrate the earth, and we saw as it were a sea of fire. Plunged in this fire were demons and souls in human form, like transparent burning embers, all blackened or burnished bronze, floating about in the conflagration, now raised into the air by the flames that issued from within themselves together with great clouds of smoke, now falling back on every side like sparks in huge fires, without weight or equilibrium, amid shrieks and groans of pain and despair, which horrified us

and made us tremble with fear…The demons could be distinguished by their terrifying and repellent likeness to frightful and unknown animals, black and transparent burning coals.[5]

The children were terrified by the vision of hell. In his theological commentary on *The Message of Fatima*, written when he was Joseph Cardinal Ratzinger, Pope Benedict XVI said:

> For one terrible moment, the children were given a vision of hell. They saw the fall of "the souls of poor sinners." And now they are told why they have been exposed to this moment: "in order to save souls"—to show the way to salvation. The words of the First Letter of Peter come to mind: "As the outcome of your faith you obtain the salvation of your souls" (1:9). To reach this goal, the way indicated…is devotion to the Immaculate Heart of Mary. A brief comment may suffice to explain this. In biblical language the "heart" indicates the center of human life, the point where reason, will, temperament and sensitivity converge, where the person finds his unity and his interior orientation. According to Matthew 5:8, the "immaculate heart" is a heart which makes the *fiat*—"your will be done"—the defining center of one's whole life. It might be objected that we should not place a human being between ourselves and Christ. But then we remember that Paul did not hesitate to say to his communities: "imitate me" [1 Corinthians 4:16; Philippians 3:17; 1 Thessalonians 1:6; 2 Thessalonians 3:7, 9]. In the Apostle they could see concretely what it meant to follow Christ. But from whom might we better learn in every age than from the Mother of the Lord?[6]

The First Secret: The Existence of Hell

The terrifying vision of hell profoundly impacted the three children. We should keep in mind that Jacinta was only seven years old, Francisco was nine, and Lucia was just ten years old at the time of

Our Lady's apparitions. They were young, innocent, and very faithful to God. The vision of hell was extremely frightening for them to see. And yet, we can appreciate that in God's Divine Providence, he allowed the children to see hell with all its very real, gory, and horrifying detail.

She also told the young visionaries how they could help to prevent people from going there. The Lady said, "To save them, God wishes to establish in the world devotion to my Immaculate Heart. If what I say to you is done, many souls will be saved and there will be peace." We will discuss more about the Immaculate Heart of Mary a little bit later. For now, we will focus on the vision of hell and the effect it had on the children.

Years later, Lucia would write about hell, saying that many people are hesitant to talk about it, especially to children. Specifically, she said, "Some people, even the most devout, refuse to speak to children about hell, in case it would frighten them. Yet God did not hesitate to show hell to three children, one of whom was only six years old, knowing well that they would be horrified to the point of...withering away with fear."[7]

Indeed, hell is not a subject that many would like to discuss. In fact, many people ignore the topic altogether. It's just too uncomfortable for them. One of the devil's biggest tricks is to persuade us not to believe in hell. On the other hand, the fear of hell can help one to stay on the straight and narrow path that leads to heaven.

Other saints, including St. Faustina Kowalska, were also shown visions of hell. In her writings, St. Faustina explicitly described the extensive chasms of hell and the great tortures she witnessed. She said she would have died at the very sight of the tortures if it were not for God supporting her. In her book, *Divine Mercy In My Soul: The Diary of the Servant of God, Sister M. Faustina Kowalska*, otherwise known simply as *The Diary*, St. Faustina testifies to the existence of hell. She says:

> Each soul undergoes terrible and indescribable sufferings, related to the manner in which it has sinned. There are caverns and pits of torture where one form of agony differs from another.... Let the sinner know that he will be tortured throughout all eternity, in those senses which he made use of to sin. I am writing this at the command of God, so that no soul may find an excuse by saying there is no hell, or that nobody has ever been there, and so no one can say what it is like.... I, Sister Faustina Kowalska, by the order of God, have visited the Abysses of Hell so that I might tell souls about it and testify to its existence.... The devils were full of hatred for me, but they had to obey me at the command of God. What I have written is but a pale shadow of the things I saw. But I noticed one thing: That most of the souls there are those who disbelieved that there is a hell.... How terribly souls suffer there! Consequently, I pray even more fervently for the conversion of sinners. I incessantly plead God's mercy upon them. O My Jesus, I would rather be in agony until the end of the world, amidst the greatest sufferings, than offend you by the least sin."[8]

Lucia, Francisco, and Jacinta were shown the reality of hell so that they could more fully understand and communicate to us the need to pray for sinners. Through their witness of the first secret, the world could believe the existence of hell. As the Blessed Mother explained to them, it was the place, "where the souls of poor sinners go."

Years later, Lucia commented on the duration and intensity of the vision of hell. She said, "This vision lasted but an instant. How could we ever be grateful enough to our kind heavenly Mother, who had already prepared us by promising, in the first Apparition, to take us to heaven. Otherwise, I think we would have died of fear and terror."[9]

The Second Secret: War, Peace, and the Immaculate Heart
Completely terrified by the vision of hell given them, Lucia and her cousins looked up at the Lady, as if to plead for succor.

With both great sadness and deep kindness, the Lady said,

> You have seen hell where souls of poor sinners go. To save them, God wishes to establish in the world devotion to my Immaculate Heart. If what I say to you is done, many souls will be saved and there will be peace.
>
> The war is going to end; but if people do not cease in offending God, a worse one will break out during the pontificate of Pius XI. When you see a night illuminated by an unknown light, know that this is the great sign given you by God that he is about to punish the world for its crimes, by means of war, famine, and persecutions of the Church and of the Holy Father."[10]

The Lady continued to speak to the three children after showing them the vision of hell. She told about terrible things that could happen, including war, calamities, and sufferings.

"To prevent this," the Lady continued, "I shall come to ask for the consecration of Russia to my Immaculate Heart, and the Communion of Reparation on the First Saturdays. If my requests are heeded, Russia will be converted, and there will be peace; if not, she will spread errors throughout the world, causing wars and persecutions of the Church. The good will be martyred, the Holy Father will have much to suffer, various nations will be annihilated."

It was a dire warning, but she also offered hope.

She said, "In the end, my Immaculate Heart will triumph. The Holy Father will consecrate Russia to me, and she will be converted, and a period of peace will be granted to the world."

More information about First Saturday Consecrations may be found in the Appendix of this book.

Renewed Fervor to Suffer for the Salvation of Souls

After showing Lucia, Francisco, and Jacinta the vision of hell, the beautiful Lady taught them a new prayer to pray at the end of each decade of the rosary. This prayer is known as the Fatima Decade Prayer.

She said, "When you pray the rosary, say after each mystery: O my Jesus, forgive us, save us from the fire of hell. Lead all souls to heaven, especially those in most need."

This is a prayer that we say today during our rosaries. God wants us to care about the salvation of others, not only of our own. In fact, we are to work out our salvation while here on earth, and we are to live our lives in such a way that we can help others get to heaven too.

The children knew without a doubt that they were needed to work tirelessly for the Lady to help save souls. They possessed a whole-hearted trust in her message to them. They were still feeling stunned by the vision of hell when Lucia, who had become the spokesperson for the three cousins, asked the Lady another question.

"Is there anything more that you want of me?"

"No, I do not want anything more of you today," she said before vanishing once again from their presence.

All three children changed their lives dramatically immediately after being shown the vision of hell. They were already pious, faith-filled children, especially after the Angel of Peace visits the previous year and the visits by the Blessed Mother. But after seeing souls suffer terribly in hell, their fervor to save souls deeply impacted all of their days. They no longer sought happiness or comfort for themselves, but instead sought to offer all they could for the salvation of souls and to console Jesus and Mary and offer prayers for the Holy Father.

Jacinta was so shaken by the vision of hell that she wished everyone could see the same vision and be convinced to turn their lives around before it was too late. Lucia later said, "Jacinta's thirst for making sacrifices seemed insatiable."[11] Little Jacinta constantly encouraged her brother and older cousin to sacrifice along with her. She cried out, "Oh, hell! Hell! How sorry I am for the souls who go to hell! And the people down there, burning alive, like wood in the fire!"[12]

Whenever Jacinta thought about hell, with all the shrieking demons and agonizing groans of those suffering, she immediately got down on her knees, shuddering over the terror of the fate of hell, and prayed fervently for sinners in her attempt to save them from being imprisoned in hell.

"O my Jesus! Forgive us, save us from the fire of hell. Lead all souls to heaven, especially those who are in most need," she prayed, just like the Lady had taught her. She made countless sacrifices along with her prayers, so steadfast was her conviction. Later we will see how she responded to the Blessed Mother when asked about the end of her life.

Francisco prayed many rosaries, as the Lady had requested of him at the first apparition in the Cova da Iria. He grew to become very close to the Eucharistic Lord, desiring to keep company with the "Hidden Jesus" in a quiet church where he could humbly offer penances, prayers, and sacrifices—alone with his Jesus.

Lucia had much to suffer, which she patiently and lovingly offered up for the poor sinners. Lucia's mother often hit her with a broom handle or would grab a stick from near the fireplace to beat her. Lucia offered any feelings of sadness to God. Her mother treated her so differently than Francisco and Jacinta's parents treated them in response to the visions.

Lucia later wrote, "By a special grace from Our Lord, I never experienced the slightest thought or feeling of resentment regarding the manner of acting towards me. As the Angel had announced that God would send me sufferings, I always saw the hand of God in it all."[13]

The crowds, which continued to grow, peppered Lucia—who had become the spokesperson with the crowds as well as the Lady—with constant questions. Peace and quiet could no longer be found in a place that had previously been nothing but serene and secluded. Moments of solitude were fleeting and often nonexistent.

Other challenges emerged. Lucia's family's land was trampled on over and over again by thousands of pilgrims traveling to the apparition site. These pilgrims were eager to pray the rosary and to somehow be part of the miraculous visits from the Lady, but their presence meant the fertile land could no longer be used for the family's livelihood. Undoubtedly, Lucia's mother was not happy. She let Lucia know about her unhappiness with harsh words and the broom shank.

Throughout all of the challenges, the three cousins grew even closer to one another in God's love. They continually encouraged one another with their prayers and love. They also tried to think of new penances and sacrifices in their deep desire to save souls for Jesus and Mary. They wore penitential ropes under their clothes, cinched tight at the waist and never complained as they offered their sufferings for heaven.

Many years later, Sister Lucia wrote,

> This call to sacrifice, which God now addresses to us, is something which we find in many pages of Sacred Scripture.... As St. Paul tells us (Colossians 1:24), we must complete in ourselves what is lacking in the Passion of Christ, because we are members of the Mystical Body.... We are all ill, we all have many defects and sins; hence we all have a duty to make sacrifices, in union with Christ, the innocent victim, in reparation for own sins and for those of our brothers and sisters, because we are all members

of the one and the same Mystical Body of the Lord.... They may be sacrifices of spiritual, intellectual, moral, physical or material things...[14]

The Third Secret: "Penance, Penance, Penance!"

The Third Secret was revealed to the children at the Cova on July 13, 1917. It was to be kept in the greatest confidence. When Sister Lucia was with the Dorothean Sisters in Tuy, Spain, she fell ill in mid-1943. Because it was feared that she could die before the Third Secret was revealed by her, the Bishop of Leiria requested that she write down the remainder of the Secret (or Third Secret) told to the children in 1917. Obediently, and in the midst of her painful sickness, Sister Lucia wrote it down on a single sheet of paper. She placed it in an envelope and sealed it.

Before we look at Sister Lucia's testimony, I offer the words of then-Cardinal Joseph Ratzinger, who gives some context to the revelations of Lucia. There was great speculation and controversy over the Third Secret of Fatima because it was kept under wraps for many years. In his *Theological Commentary* on *The Message of Fatima*, Cardinal Ratzinger pointed out that the contents of the envelope that held the Third Secret for so long might be "disappointing" to some.

A careful reading of the text of the so-called third "secret" of Fatima, published here in its entirety long after the fact and by decision of the Holy Father, will probably prove disappointing or surprising after all the speculation it has stirred. No great mystery is revealed; nor is the future unveiled. We see the Church of the martyrs of the century which has just passed represented in a scene described in a language which is symbolic and not easy to decipher. Is this what the Mother of the Lord wished to communicate to Christianity and to humanity at a time of great difficulty and distress? Is it of any help to us at the beginning of the new millennium? Or are these only projections of the inner world of children, brought up in a climate of profound piety but shaken at the same time by the tempests which threatened their own time? How should we understand the vision? What are we to make of it?[15]

Cardinal Ratzinger discussed the "secret" of Fatima in depth in *The Message of Fatima*, the full text of which is available online on the Vatican website. For now, we focus on his words:

> And so we come to the final question: What is the meaning of the 'secret' of Fatima as a whole (in its three parts)? What does it say to us? First of all, we must affirm with Cardinal Sodano: "...the events to which the third part of the 'secret' of Fatima refers now seem part of the past." Insofar as individual events are described, they belong to the past. Those who expected exciting apocalyptic revelations about the end of the world or the future course of history are bound to be disappointed. Fatima does not satisfy our curiosity in this way, just as Christian faith in general cannot be reduced to an object of mere curiosity. What remains was already evident when we began our reflections on the text of the "secret": the exhortation to prayer as the path of "salvation for souls" and, likewise, the summons to penance and conversion.[16]

Now let us look at what happened and what the three young shepherds witnessed. As discussed above, in 1943, Sister Lucia, under obedience to God, the Bishop of Leiria, and the Blessed Mother, wrote the following description of the third part of the secret revealed to her and her two cousins on July 13, 1917:

> J.M.J.
> The third part of the secret revealed at the Cova da Iria-Fatima, on 13 July 1917.
>
> I write in obedience to you, my God, who command me to do

so through his Excellency the Bishop of Leiria and through your Most Holy Mother and mine.

After the two parts which I have already explained, at the left of Our Lady and a little above, we saw an Angel with a flaming sword in his left hand; flashing, it gave out flames that looked as though they would set the world on fire; but they died out in contact with the splendor that Our Lady radiated towards him from her right hand: pointing to the earth with his right hand, the Angel cried out in a loud voice: "*Penance, Penance, Penance!*" And we saw in an immense light that is God: "something similar to how people appear in a mirror when they pass in front of it" a Bishop dressed in White "we had the impression that it was the Holy Father". Other Bishops, Priests, men and women Religious going up a steep mountain, at the top of which there was a big Cross of rough-hewn trunks as of a cork-tree with the bark; before reaching there the Holy Father passed through a big city half in ruins and half trembling with halting step, afflicted with pain and sorrow, he prayed for the souls of the corpses he met on his way; having reached the top of the mountain, on his knees at the foot of the big Cross he was killed by a group of soldiers who fired bullets and arrows at him, and in the same way there died one after another the other Bishops, Priests, men and women Religious, and various lay people of different ranks and positions. Beneath the two arms of the Cross there were two Angels each with a crystal aspersorium in his hand, in which they gathered up the blood of the Martyrs and with it sprinkled the souls that were making their way to God.[17]

The scenes that Sister Lucia recalled are intense and wildly descriptive. We can only imagine what the three young visionaries experienced and thought upon receiving the great prophetic secrets of Fatima that day. The words and visions given by God and the Blessed Mother are meant for all of us.

Sister Lucia's Interpretation of the Third Secret

Almost forty years later, in a May 1982 letter to the Holy Father, Sister Lucia gave an interpretation of the Third Secret. She wrote:

> The third part of the secret refers to Our Lady's words: "If not [Russia] will spread her errors throughout the world, causing wars and persecutions of the Church. The good will be martyred; the Holy Father will have much to suffer; various nations will be annihilated."[18]
>
> The third part of the secret is a symbolic revelation, referring to this part of the Message, conditioned by whether we accept or not what the Message itself asks of us: "If my requests are heeded, Russia will be converted, and there will be peace; if not, she will spread her errors throughout the world, etc."
>
> Since we did not heed this appeal of the Message, we see that it has been fulfilled, Russia has invaded the world with her errors. And if we have not yet seen the complete fulfillment of the final part of this prophecy, we are going towards it little by little with great strides. If we do not reject the path of sin, hatred, revenge, injustice, violations of the rights of the human person, immorality and violence, etc.
>
> And let us not say that it is God who is punishing us in this way; on the contrary it is people themselves who are preparing their own punishment. In his kindness God warns us and calls us to the right path, while respecting the freedom he has given us; hence people are responsible."[19]

At long last the Third Secret of Fatima was revealed. We learn from the Congregation for the Doctrine of the Faith:

> The decision of His Holiness Pope John Paul II to make public the third part of the "secret" of Fatima brings to an end a period of history marked by tragic human lust for power and evil, yet

pervaded by the merciful love of God and the watchful care of the Mother of Jesus and of the Church.

The action of God, the Lord of history, and the co-responsibility of man in the drama of his creative freedom, are the two pillars upon which human history is built.

Our Lady, who appeared at Fatima, recalls these forgotten values. She reminds us that man's future is in God, and we are active and responsible partners in creating that future.[20]

Pope John Paul II and the Third Secret

As was noted earlier, the envelope containing the Third Secret was not to be opened before 1960. Sister Lucia had asked her Bishop of Leiria to read it but he refused. Instead, it was given to him for safekeeping, and later, to ensure better protection, it was placed in the Secret Archives of the Holy Office on April 4, 1957.

On August 17, 1959, Fr. Pierre Paul Philippe, OP, the commissary of the Holy Office, with the agreement of Cardinal Alfredo Ottaviani, brought the envelope which contained the Third Secret of Fatima to Pope John XXIII. According to the *Message of Fatima*, Pope John XXIII hesitated and said, "We shall wait. I shall pray. I shall let you know what I decide."[21]

Pope John XXIII decided not to reveal the "secret" and returned the envelope to the Holy Office. Almost six years later, on March 27, 1965, Pope Paul VI read the contents and decided not to publish it. The envelope was then returned to the Archives of the Holy Office.

Not long after he was seriously wounded in a burst of gunfire in St. Peter's Square, Pope John Paul II requested the envelope containing the third part of the secret. The pontiff had written a message to be read to pilgrims in Fatima to commemorate the anniversary of the apparitions. Astonishingly, this message was being read aloud on May 13, 1981 at the moment Mehmet Ali Agca fired shots at the pope, who was standing in an open car moving slowly into St. Peter's Square, which was filled with more than ten thousand people.

Pope John Paul II was shot four times and suffered severe blood loss. He was near death when he arrived at Gemelli Hospital. His very first thoughts were on Fatima when he regained consciousness. He began to read Sister Lucia's *Memoirs* and her letters during his months of recuperation at the hospital. The recovery was slow going, but the pontiff knew what he needed to read next. On July 18, Pope John Paul II asked for the envelope containing the Third Secret of Fatima.

Cardinal Franjo Seper, prefect of the Congregation, gave two envelopes to Archbishop Eduardo Martinez Somalo, substitute of the Secretariat of State, to be delivered to the pontiff. One was a white envelope which contained Sister Lucia's original writing in Portuguese. The other envelope was orange and contained the Italian translation of the "secret." The two envelopes were returned to the Archives of the Holy Office on August 11, 1981, after a thorough review by Pope John Paul II.

The Holy Father was very moved upon reading the contents of the envelope as the reality of the "secret" sunk deeper into his heart. He immediately thought of consecrating the world to the Immaculate Heart of Mary. He believed that on May 13, 1981, which was the sixty-fourth anniversary of the first apparition in Fatima, the Blessed Mother guided the bullets that shot him to protect him from death. The Third Secret of Fatima was so much about him, the "Bishop dressed in white." Pope John Paul II recognized himself as the pope (or bishop) who, in the third part of the secret, was killed. However, Pope John Paul II was not killed, but was miraculously saved by the Blessed Mother.

Some would later say that Pope John Paul II couldn't possibly be the "Bishop in white" in the vision because he did not die. To that,

Pope John Paul II answered that he should have died but the Blessed Mother brought him back from the brink of death. He even went so far as to say that the Blessed Mother gave him back his life. There was no question in his mind.

Controversy over the Third Secret

The Third Secret of Our Lady of Fatima was made public on May 13, 2000, at the beatification Mass of Francisco and Jacinta Marto. The Mass was held in the Cova da Iria, where Our Lady told the young shepherds the three secrets.

As soon as the Third Secret was revealed, controversies spread like wildfire. Many questioned whether or not the Vatican was holding back the full secret. Was the Church revealing the authentic text? Where were the words about an impending great apostasy, a warning of a nuclear holocaust, or about Satan entering the Church? People wanted to believe that the Third Secret was about impending disasters. As Cardinal Ratzinger predicted, many were disappointed once the secret was revealed, and for some, disappointment led to suspicion. Many conspiracy theories surfaced.

In the document *The Message of Fatima* by the Congregation for the Doctrine of the Faith, Archbishop Bertone stated: "There is only one manuscript, which is here reproduced photostatically." Sister Lucia also confirmed the Vatican text. She met with Archbishop Bertone and Bishop Seraphim de Sousa of Leiria at her Carmelite convent in Coimbra, Portugal, on April 27, 2000. Two envelopes were presented to her by the Archbishop. The first envelope was the outer envelope containing the second envelope which held the Third Secret.

Sister Lucia touched the letter and stated, "This is my letter." She then read it and said, "This is my writing." She was asked if it was the only Third Secret. She said, "Yes, this is the Third Secret, and I never wrote another."[22]

On November 17, 2001, Sister Lucia met again with Archbishop Bertone. A Vatican Secret Service communiqué about their meeting, dated December 20, 2001, and titled "Sister Lucy: Secret of Fatima Contains No More Mysteries" states:

> With reference to the third part of the secret of Fatima, [Sister Lucia] affirmed that she had attentively read and meditated upon the booklet published by the Congregation for the Doctrine of the Faith [*The Message of Fatima*] and confirmed everything that was written there. To whoever imagines that some part of the secret has been hidden, she replied: "Everything has been published; no secret remains." To those who speak and write of new revelations, she said: "There is no truth in this. If I received new revelations, I would have told no one, but I would have communicated them directly to the Holy Father."

Our minds and hearts should be at complete ease knowing that before her death, Sister Lucia made absolutely sure that Our Lady's words and messages were revealed to the world at the proper time, and that the consecration of the world—including Russia to Mary's Immaculate Heart—was fully made appropriately to satisfy the Blessed Mother.

A Time to Reflect

The Blessed Mother revealed quite a lot in the third apparition at Fatima. Because of it, all three children changed their lives dramatically after being shown the vision of hell. We know that they were already pious, faith-filled children. But after seeing the horrific suffering in hell, their fervor to save souls deeply impacted all of their days. They no longer sought happiness or comfort for themselves, but instead sought to offer all they could for the salvation of souls and to console Jesus and Mary and offer prayers for the Holy Father.

Do we do the same? Do we understand the great importance to help them? The Blessed Mother herself requests this help from us.

In My Own Life

Take some time soon to ponder where your life is going. Are you on a sort of treadmill of life? Do you seek a conversion of heart each and every day? We must not become stagnant in our faith. As well, we must not be afraid to talk about the reality of hell which is a punishment for sin.

We live in a convoluted world full of fear about what lies ahead. Yet, we have promises of heaven and peace of heart if we follow the commandments and strive for holiness. We must be a light to others in a darkened world. We must pray for the graces to be more generous with our time so that we can offer many prayers, offerings, and sacrifices for those who are in need.

We don't want to let the devil snatch our brothers and sisters to the terrors of hell. Let's pray for them now while there is time.

Prayer

Dear Lord God, please grant me the graces to remain faithful to your commandments. Help me in every way to turn my life fully towards you and not to get caught up with the evil allurements of the world. Please, dear Mother Mary, take me close to your Immaculate Heart to keep me safe and help me to selflessly offer many prayers and sacrifices for sinners. All of the angels and saints, please pray for me. Amen.

Chapter Five

The Fourth and Fifth Apparitions of Fatima

At a time when the human family was ready to sacrifice all that was most sacred on the altar of the petty and selfish interests of nations, races, ideologies, groups and individuals, our Blessed Mother came from heaven, offering to implant in the hearts of all those who trust in her the Love of God burning in her own heart.[1]

The August Apparition Delayed

Word about the apparitions at Fatima was speeding like wildfire throughout the regions of Portugal. The children made known that the Lady had promised a miracle in October, and that she had also confided some important secrets to them. Scores of people were intrigued, while plenty of others were mocking.

Even the secular press began to report on the happenings. Since many of the reporters were anti-religious, they wrote critical articles calling the believers "religious fanatics" and the like, and blaming administrators for not putting a stop to the fiasco.[2]

A local chief official named Artur de Oliveira Santos was a Freemason and very anti-Catholic. He took the reporter's criticisms personally and set out to discredit the children, hoping to prove that the visions and apparitions were a hoax, and to stop the enormous crowds from descending upon the apparition site.

Administrator Santos was suspicious of the "secrets" and tried to force information out of the children with threats and scare tactics. He arranged for the children and their parents to meet at his headquarters in Ourem. Lucia went with her father but Ti Marto went alone. He would not allow his children to walk nine miles to get there. Lucia stopped in to see Jacinta and Francisco briefly before the journey.

Lucia later revealed in her *Memoirs* that the children believed they might be put to death, or at least Lucia might be. She said:

> As we were passing by my uncle's house, my father had to wait a few minutes for my uncle. I ran to say good-bye to Jacinta who was still in bed. Doubtful as to whether we would ever see one another again, I threw my arms around her. Bursting into tears, the poor child sobbed:
>
> "If they kill you, tell them that Francisco and I are just the same as you, and that we want to die too. I'm going right now to the well [where the Angel of Peace appeared the second time] with Francisco, and we'll pray hard for you."[3]

Administrator Santos shamelessly interrogated Lucia, demanding that she recant and admit that it was all a hoax. He tried to get her to promise that she would not go back to the apparition site. He further threatened to have her killed if she didn't do as he told her. But little Lucia would not budge. Administrator Santos threatened that the parents of all three would be punished civilly if they did not stop them from going to the Cova da Iria.

As August 13, 1917, approached, more pilgrims than ever before were making their way to the Cova da Iria. But Administrator Santos had a trick up his sleeve. He and a priest from a neighboring parish showed up unannounced at the homes of the visionaries on the morning of August 13. He told the families that he wanted to be like St. Thomas and believe by *seeing*. He said he wanted to take the children to the apparition site after a meeting with the children's pastor. He would take them all in his own horse-drawn wagon. Believing him, the children went with the administrator.

But the lying Santos turned the wagon towards Ourem, not the parish. He had tricked the families and the innocent children. He ordered the wagon to stop at his home where his wife, who practiced her Catholic faith without her husband's knowledge, served the children lunch before heading to the city hall. Upon reaching the city hall, the children were once again questioned about the apparitions and the great secret. They were kept late and subsequently had to stay overnight at the home of the administrator and his wife.

The next morning, Administrator Santos ordered that the children be arrested. The young visionaries were taken to jail and interrogated. These children—all under the age of eleven, remember—were surrounded by true criminals and began to fear that their parents had abandoned them.

Little Jacinta said, "Neither your parents nor mine have come to see us. They don't bother about us anymore!" Then she burst out crying.

Francisco, as a caring big brother, reminded her, "Don't cry. We can offer this to Jesus for sinners." Francisco then raised his eyes and hands heavenward and said, "Oh my Jesus, this is for love of you, and for the conversion of sinners."

Jacinta perked up and chimed in, "And also for the Holy Father, and in reparation for the sins committed against the Immaculate Heart of Mary."[4]

All three children were courageous, even through tears. They were heroically willing to go to their death before divulging the secret. Seeing their predicament, the prisoners suggested that the children simply tell what they knew and get out of jail.

"Never!" Jacinta retorted. "I'd rather die!"

Many years later, Lucia would write:

Jacinta took off a medal that she was wearing around her neck, and asked a prisoner to hang it up for her on a nail in the hall.

Kneeling before this medal, we began to pray. The prisoners prayed with us, that is, if they knew how to pray, but at least they were down on their knees.... While we were saying the rosary in prison, [Francisco] noticed that one of the prisoners was on his knees with his cap still on his head. Francisco went right up to him and said, "If you wish to pray, you should take your cap off." Right away, the poor man handed it to him and he went over and put it on the bench on top of his own.[5]

Even in the midst of the fear and uncertainty, there was a short time of dancing in the jail cell. One of the prisoners started playing his concertina and others sang songs. The children danced with the thieves. This was certainly not a scene that Administrator Santos expected to see.

Santos had the children brought out of the cell so that he could again interrogate and intimidate them. This was a great trial for the children, who were questioned separately. But the young cousins refused to divulge what the Lady had entrusted to them. Santos then threatened that it was against the law to withhold information from him, but the young visionaries stood firm and courageously refused.

Jacinta was questioned first. We can only imagine what Lucia and Francisco were thinking when little Jacinta was snatched from them and subjected to the interrogation. Jacinta was the youngest to be put through this horrible ordeal. Yet, strong-willed Jacinta stood firm and would not reveal the secret to the administrator, no matter his threats or demands.

When he realized he couldn't get anything out of the child, Santos called a guard and asked if the oil was boiling. The guard responded affirmatively, and Santos said he should throw her in the cauldron! The guard grabbed little Jacinta to escort her to her death in boiling oil.

Francisco was next. He too remained strong and courageous through frightening interrogations, knowing that he could be boiled in oil too. He said he would rather die than reveal the Lady's secret. He was immediately escorted out of the room by the guard.

Lucia was now left alone with Administrator Santos and the guards. For all Lucia knew, her cousins and companions through the ordeal had been brutally killed in the next room. Still, she remained steadfast. The relentless questioning commenced. Lucia refused to tell the Lady's secret, saying she preferred death, for after which she would go to heaven. She too was taken out of the room.

To her joy and relief, her younger cousins were waiting for her, alive and safe. The threats had been hollow, and the children were physically unharmed. Yet, there was a sense of sadness amid the joy because they realized it was not their time to go to heaven.

Though glad to be alive and together again, their imprisonment kept them far away from the Cova during the time the Lady had promised another visit.

Would the Lady be disappointed? What would unfold next?

Where Is the Lady?

While the administrator had the children detained on August 13, thousands of people had traveled to the Cova for the Lady's appearance. The pilgrims wondered why the children were not there. They stayed and prayed at the apparition site for a while. But it was not the same without the children, though some sensed that certain mystical signs were occurring as in the past. The day passed, and there was still no sign of the shepherd children. The confused crowd finally left the Cova, very disappointed.

On August 15, the Solemnity of the Assumption of the Blessed Virgin Mary into Heaven, Administrator Santos finally freed the children from prison. They were dropped off at the parish rectory. The rectory and surrounding areas were busy as Mass was getting out on the special feast day, and many witnessed the children being dropped off. The people were furious as they came to understand that the children had been abducted. Ti Marto, Francisco and Jacinta's father, intervened to stop fights right there at the church. As upset as he was about what had happened, he said the Lord allowed the ordeal to take place. We can consider that God must have granted him graces to understand the situation and calm the people.

The children were very happy to finally return home. Francisco and Jacinta were showered with great affection, while Lucia was treated as if nothing had happened to her. Lucia accepted her mother's behavior as a penance and did not resent her for it. Later on she would say her ability to do so was a special grace from God.

August 19, 1917

Lucia, Francisco, and his brother John took the sheep out to graze on Sunday, August 19. Jacinta stayed home. This day they were at a place called Valinhos just a short walk from their hamlet of Aljustrel. Lucia sensed that the Lady was coming.

At about four o'clock a flash of light like lightening appeared. It was so very familiar. But, could the Lady be coming without Jacinta? Lucia was concerned and asked John to run back to get her, but John said he didn't want to go back. Lucia resorted to paying him a couple of pennies to fetch little Jacinta. When Jacinta arrived at the site where the others awaited, the Lady immediately appeared, standing upon a holm oak tree. It was the first time that the Lady came to this place and not the Cova.

Lucia immediately posed her usual question, "What do you want of me?"

The Lady responded: "I want you to continue going to the Cova da Iria on the thirteenth, and to continue praying the rosary every day. In the last month, I will perform a miracle so that all may believe."

The Lady's words and countenance brought peace and comfort. She continued to emphasize the importance of praying the rosary for peace and to save souls. She again told them that she would perform a miracle, promising to do so in October.

Lucia then asked, "What are we to do with the offerings of money that people leave at the Cova da Iria?"

The Blessed Mother told her, "Have two litters made. One is to be carried by you and Jacinta and two other girls dressed in white; the other one is to be carried by Francisco and three other boys. The money from the litters is for the 'fiesta' of Our Lady of the Rosary, and what is left over will help towards the construction of a chapel that is to be built here."[6]

The litters would be used to carry statues during the procession on October 7, the feast of Our Lady of the Rosary. The Lady was asking that the donations be used to make the litters and afterwards to help with the construction of a chapel. Later on, Lucia would explain to the archbishop that the litters would be used to carry around the pilgrim statues of Our Lady of Fatima. We will discuss the pilgrim statues later on.

Lucia asked the Lady for a healing for some sick people. The Lady answered, "Some I will cure during the year." Lucia would later recount how the Lady's face suddenly took on a very sad appearance. Then the Lady said, "Pray, pray very much, and make sacrifices for sinners; for many souls go to hell, because there are none to sacrifice themselves and to pray for them."[7]

The children felt very impacted by the Lady's sad face and reminder to constantly pray and make sacrifices. The thought of souls going to hell because there was no one to pray and sacrifice resounded in their hearts.

September 13, 1917

There was much hubbub because of the recent abduction and imprisonment of the children. Folks had been talking continuously. There were many stories circulating about the heavenly visits and the faithful and courageous shepherd children.

Countless people were coming from far and wide, desiring even a small glimpse of what was going on for themselves. There were those who were simply curious, but there were also plenty who sincerely believed and who were hopeful. Many priests could be seen in the crowd. They would later testify in favor of the apparitions which contributed to the investigation done by the Church.

By the time the cousins headed out to the Cova on the morning of September 13, all of the roads leading there were clogged with people. The children had trouble getting to the Cova themselves because of the throngs of people—all calling out to them when they recognized the young visionaries. There was an estimated twenty-five thousand people there that day. A kind stranger helped the children get to where the Lady would appear by carving a passage through the crowd ahead of them.

Along the way, many people begged assistance from the children. People threw themselves before them, some on their knees and begging for prayers. Others shouted to them from a distance. They knew that the children could communicate with the heavenly Lady, and they desperately desired cures and answers to their prayers.

Lucia said, "They threw themselves on their knees before us, begging us to place their petitions before Our Lady.... All the afflictions of poor humanity were assembled there."[8]

The determined children finally arrived at the spot of the apparitions and knelt to pray the rosary. After the rosary, the familiar flash of light occurred, and immediately the Lady was above the holm oak tree. The Lady would reveal some amazing things to come.

Lucia was always eager to come to the Lady's assistance. "What do you want of me?" she asked.

"Continue to pray the rosary in order to obtain an end of the war. In October Our Lord will come, as well as Our Lady of Dolours [Sorrows] and Our Lady of Carmel. Saint Joseph will appear with the Child Jesus to bless the world. God is pleased with your sacrifices. He does not want you to sleep with the rope on, but only wear it during the daytime."

They had been faithfully praying the daily rosary, saying the special prayers they were taught, and making many sacrifices for reparation. They had decided to wear a rope around their waist to offer a secret, painful sacrifice to God. But God is a sensible and loving God, and though he was pleased with their sacrifices, he told them through the Blessed Mother at the apparition that they should sleep restfully at night and not with the extra pain.

Lucia felt it important to ask for help from the Lady for all the people who had pleaded with her along the road. She said, "I was told to ask you many things, the cure of some sick people, of a deaf-mute…"

"Yes, I will cure some, but not others. In October I will perform a miracle so that all may believe."

The Lady departed. Lucia suddenly pointed towards the east and cried out, "If you want to see our Lady, look there!" Some testified later that they saw something luminous like a cloud that transported the Lady.

Now the children as well as the tens of thousands of people who were interested in the apparitions in the Cova would have to wait another month to see if the Lady would come through with her promise to show a sign, some kind of a miracle. The children had no doubt whatsoever that the holy Lady would deliver what she had been promising.

For the children, it would be a month filled with praying, sacrificing, dealing with unending questions, and waiting as patiently as possible for the Lady to prove herself.

A TIME TO REFLECT

We see that the children went through many challenges because they were faithful to the Blessed Mother's instructions and requests. Even though they lacked years in which to learn courage, they were more brave than many adults would be in their situation. We can learn so much from their faithful example.

IN MY OWN LIFE

Was there a time in your life when everything went completely wrong? Were you ever so frightened that you weren't sure what to do? Can you learn from three little shepherd children how to be faithful and trusting of God? He stays with us even in the dark corners of life. He is with us even when we don't know what to do. He awaits our prayers.

PRAYER

Dear Father God, please stay with me always. Help me to stay faithful to you and never turn my back on you. Dear Holy Spirit, please enlighten me. Dear Jesus and Mary, help me to be an example of God's love to all I meet. St. Joseph and all of the angels and saints, please pray for me. Amen.

Chapter Six

THE MIRACLE OF THE DANCING SUN

If the Lady doesn't do the miracle the people will attack us, so we had better go to confession and be properly prepared for death.[1]

People desiring to be present at the Cova da Iria for the October 13 visit from the Lady were coming to the area like herds of hungry sheep setting out for a new pasture. They were traveling from far and wide in cars, wagons, and on foot, earnestly motivated to see a miracle. Still others were full of mockery, convinced that nothing spectacular would happen.

Certainly, the day did not start off looking like a miracle would occur. Instead, the weather was devilishly gloomy as the rain that had begun days earlier continued to pound down with a vengeance, creating sucking mud and gaping puddles for the pilgrims to trudge through. Yet, the mud and rain didn't dampen spirits. The pilgrims came in droves, praying along the way, even singing, despite the miserable conditions. It is estimated that forty thousand to eighty thousand people were at the Cova that day. In addition, approximately twenty thousand more stood on hillsides and beyond, trying to observe the proceedings from as far away as twenty-five miles.

That morning, Lucia's mother, Maria Rosa, sprang up from sleep. She had an intense need to go to the sacrament of confession with her young daughter.

"Lucia, we had better go to confession," she said. "Everyone says that we shall probably be killed tomorrow in the Cova da Iria." There was no mincing words here. Maria Rosa had no time to waste. "If the Lady doesn't do the miracle, the people will attack us, so we had better go to confession and be properly prepared for death."

Lucia was not worried about death. Truth be told, she longed for heaven. But she was very confident that it wouldn't be today. The Lady would come through with her promises.

Lucia had no doubts. Over the past year she had been prepared by heaven. With each apparition from the Angel of Peace and all of those from the Blessed Mother, Lucia, Francisco, and Jacinta were receiving graces and instruction. They grew in unfathomable, bold holiness as they prayed and sacrificed for heaven's sake.

Maria Rosa decided to go to the Cova with Lucia. "If my child is going to die, I want to die with her!"[2]

They headed out in the storm to confession. Lucia's father decided to join them. The rain was coming down in buckets. Afterwards, they went over to the Martos' house early, expecting huge crowds along the way to the Cova.

The family was not at all prepared to see the mobs of people descending upon the Martos' home. The pilgrims wanted to get close to the visionaries on such a special day. Some were there to tell them not to go to the Cova because they feared that they would be killed by angry crowds. The scene was chaotic. We can understand the bedlam through Ti Marto's own words:

> The people filled our little house so that you could not move an inch. Outside it was raining so heavily you could not see through the thickness of the falling water. Everywhere mud covered the ground.
>
> Inside the house, the people were inconsiderate and wild with their fervor and their curiosity. With their muddy shoes they climbed on the furniture, and stood without apology on the beds. My poor wife! I remember her distress at this, but there was

nothing we could do. I said to her, "Never mind, wife; at least it cannot get worse, for it is so crowded now that nobody else could possibly get in!"[3]

A woman they knew from the town of Pambalinho arrived and gently pushed her way in through the people to bring beautiful dresses for the girls to wear to see the Lady. After everyone was dressed and ready, they made their way to the Cova. While on the road, they met up with the cynical and the devout. The little group of visionaries and parents were eager to get to the apparition site, but it seemed nearly impossible to get through the dense crowds of pilgrims pressing in from every side.

As they moved closer to where Mary had been appearing at the holm oak tree, scores of people were calling out to them, pleading and pulling at the children's hearts. It was even more intense than before as the soaking wet people again dropped to their knees and begged for heavenly assistance, hoping against all hope that the children would seek it from the Lady for them. Lucia would later recall, "Not even the muddy roads could prevent these people from kneeling in the most humble and suppliant of attitudes."[4]

Ti Marto described the scene: "They kept crowding closer and getting more emotional, as though these little children had the power of saints."

The determined group pressed on through walls of people and finally, after a long and strenuous journey, arrived at the Cova da Iria. Ti Marto later recalled, "The crowd was so thick that we could not pass through. A man who was a chauffeur picked up my Jacinta at this time and carried her into the field, shouting, 'Make way for the children who saw our Lady!'"

Finally, the chauffeur who carried Jacinta reached the little oak tree and placed her down. Ti Marto said the crush of people "was so great and frightening that Jacinta began to cry. Francisco and Lucia managed then to make their way." They made it safely to the holm oak tree, but not before a man in the crowd tried to hit Ti Marto with a big stick. God's Providence through a protective group of pilgrims surrounded the assailant and prevented the attack.[5]

The "Lady of the Rosary" Appears

Upon reaching the Cova, there was no sign of the storm ending, but Lucia felt moved by an interior impulse to instruct the people to close their umbrellas and pray the rosary. The familiar flash of light appeared, and the Lady was there above the tree.

Lucia asked her usual question, "What do you want of me?"

The Lady was very specific: "I want to tell you that a chapel is to be built here in my honor. I am the Lady of the Rosary. Continue always to pray the rosary every day. The war is going to end, and the soldiers will soon return to their homes."[6]

In just those four sentences, the Blessed Mother revealed a tremendous message, with so much for the children to take in. What was Lucia to think about building a chapel? That is a very tall order for a ten-year-old to carry out!

Lucia spoke up once again with another question. "I have many things to ask you: the cure of some sick persons, the conversion of sinners, and other things..."

The Lady of the Rosary quickly answered, "Some yes, but not others. They must amend their lives and ask forgiveness for their sins."

The Lady appeared very sad as she continued, "Do not offend the Lord our God anymore, because he is already so much offended."[7]

The Blessed Mother's pure and Immaculate Heart has always keenly felt the Lord's suffering. She witnessed her Son during his public ministry being rejected by the very people he helped. The Blessed Mother was very aware of every crack of the whip that scourged her Son, mercilessly tearing away his flesh. Every pounding of the hammer to drive the nails through her Son's sacred hands and feet sent agonizing spasms of pain through Mary's whole being.

This holy Mother had never once abandoned her Son Jesus. She followed him all the way to the Cross and beyond. Her Immaculate Heart suffers when God is offended by our sins. We can be assured that the Blessed Mother cooperates fully with the redemption of the world. At the October apparition she asked that God be not offended any longer. This was a message not only for the children but for the whole world.

The Miracle of the Sun and Private Visions

The beautiful Lady then opened her hands and began to ascend. Her hands immediately reflected on the sun. Lucia explains it precisely:

> Then, opening her hands, she made them reflect on the sun, and as she ascended, the reflection of her own light continued to be projected on the sun itself. Here…is the reason why I cried out to the people to look at the sun. My aim was not to call their attention to the sun, because I was not even aware of their presence. I was moved to do so under the guidance of an interior impulse.[8]

Right at the start of this apparition, the children became unaware of everything around them—the weather, the people, the noise and crush of the crowd. They were totally fixed on the Blessed Mother speaking to them and then the opening of her hands to the miraculous light that reflected on the sun. Lucia was moved to cry out to the people to look at the sun even though she had not planned to utter a single word. But it was God's holy will that she did because what happened next is what is referred to as the "Great Miracle of the Sun."

More than fifty thousand devout, skeptical, and curious people gathered at the Cova, and those watching from afar, experienced something overwhelmingly miraculous. While that was happening, the young visionaries were seeing something else utterly amazing, but quite different, in private visions. We will get to that soon. First, we will look at some eyewitness testimonies.

As she promised, the Lady performed a great miracle for the throngs of people at the Cova da Iria. Many eyewitnesses later testified about the miracle. As well, the local secular newspapers reported on it. Approximately fifty-five thousand people in the Cova watched the extraordinary phenomenon occur. Another twenty thousand people saw the miracle within an approximate twenty-five-mile radius. It was the miracle predicted by the Lady three months prior in July. The mysterious heavenly Lady had told the children that she would reveal who she was and would perform a miracle so that the people would believe. The Lady who we now know for certain is the Blessed Mother indeed came through on her word like she said she would.

What the crowds saw was the sun doing crazy things. First, the rain stopped abruptly, and the sun grew luminously brighter. The sun started to spin and shoot beams of light, causing everything to turn different colors. But it was not a rainbow that people were seeing. The sun increased in size as if it were being hurled towards the earth. People felt sure that there was no escaping death at this point and dropped to their knees praying fervently and crying out to God for forgiveness. Even the skeptical and cynical suddenly found reason to pray.

Many testified later on that they could stare into the sun without any pain or harm to their eyes. When the sun stopped dancing and spinning, it went back to its usual place in the heavens and everything on earth, which had been thick with mud moments before, was dry. People were amazed, crying out, "Miracle! This is a miracle!"

Ti Marto testified:

> We looked easily at the sun, which for some reason did not blind us. It seemed to flicker on and off, first one way, then another. It cast its rays in many directions and painted everything in different colors—the trees, the people, the air and the ground. But what was most extraordinary, I thought, was that the sun did not hurt our eyes. Everything was still and quiet, and everyone was looking up. Then at a certain moment, the sun appeared to stop spinning. It then began to move and to dance in the sky until it seemed to detach itself from its place and fall upon us. It was a terrible moment.[9]

One eyewitness named Dr. Almeida Garrett, a professor at the University of Coimbra, gave this account:

> The sun had broken jubilantly through the thick layer of clouds just for a few moments before. It was shining clearly and intensely.... The sun was not opaque, veiled or diffused. It gave light and heat and was brightly outlined by a beveled rim.... It was a wonder that all this time it was possible for us to look at the sun, a blaze of light and burning heat, without any pain to the eyes or blinding of the retina.... [The sun] was rotating upon itself with exceedingly great speed. Suddenly, the people broke out with a cry of extreme anguish. The sun, still rotating, had unloosened itself from the skies and came hurtling towards the earth. This huge, fiery millstone threatened to crush us with its weight. It was a dreadful sensation."[10]

Avelino de Almeida, a reporter for the popular and widely read newspaper *O Seculo*, which had previously published articles mocking the apparitions, now published an article reporting on the Miracle of the Sun on October 13, 1917. The incredulous reporter made a point to be present that day. Here is an excerpt from his story:

From the road, where the vehicles were parked and where hundreds of people who had not dared to brave the mud were congregated, one could see the immense multitude turn towards the sun, which appeared free from clouds and in its zenith. It looked like a plaque of dull silver, and it was possible to look at it without the least discomfort. It might have been an eclipse which was taking place. But at that moment a great shout went up, and one could hear the spectators nearest at hand shouting: "A miracle! A miracle!"...

Before the astonished eyes of the crowd whose aspect was biblical as they stood bareheaded, eagerly searching the sky, the sun trembled, made sudden incredible movements outside all cosmic laws—the sun "danced" according to the typical expression of the people.... Standing on the step of an omnibus was an old man. With his face turned to the sun, he recited the Creed in a loud voice. I asked who he was; I saw him afterwards going up to those around him who still had their hats on, and vehemently imploring them to uncover their heads before such an extraordinary demonstration of the existence of God.... People then began to ask each other what they had seen. The great majority admitted to having seen the trembling and the dancing of the sun; others affirmed they saw the face of the Blessed Virgin; others again, swore that the sun whirled on itself like a giant wheel and that it lowered itself to the earth as if to burn it in its rays. Some said they saw it change colors successively..."[11]

In addition to newspaper reports, hundreds have given recorded formal testimony to the great Miracle of the Sun on October 13, 1917, all attesting to the authenticity of the miracle, stating that it was indeed heaven-sent. John de Marchi, in his book *Fatima: From the Beginning*, commented on the vast differences in the onlookers gathered, but none denying the miracle:

It must be admitted that this was not an afternoon of celestial fireworks enjoyed by simple and unlettered people predisposed to accept any flash of lightning as the Lord's own signal. The 70,000 witnesses included believers and non-believers, pious old ladies and scoffing young men. Hundreds, from these mixed categories, have given formal testimony. Reports do vary; impressions are in minor details confused, but none to our knowledge has directly denied the visible prodigy of the sun's unscheduled behavior in the sky.[12]

Archbishop Fulton Sheen made note of the Blessed Mother's powerful Miracle of the Sun in his book *The World's First Love*. He said:

> At Fatima, the fact that Mary could take this great center and seat of atomic power and make it her plaything, the fact that she could swing the sun "like a trinket at her wrist," is proof that God has given her power over it, not for death, but for light and life and hope. As Scripture foretold: "And now, in heaven, a great portent appeared; a woman that wore the sun for her mantle" (Revelation 12:1)."[13]

What the Children Saw

While the Miracle of the Sun was occurring, the young visionaries were privy to their own miracles in the form of visions. As was touched upon earlier, when the Blessed Mother was about to leave the children and had opened her hands to reflect upon the sun, the children beheld holy wonders. Lucia described it in her *Memoirs*. She wrote:

> After our Lady had disappeared into the immense distance of the firmament, we beheld St. Joseph with the Child Jesus and Our Lady robed in white with the blue mantle, beside the sun. St. Joseph and the Child Jesus appeared to bless the world, for

they traced the Sign of the Cross with their hands. When a little later, this apparition disappeared, I saw Our Lord and Our Lady; it seemed to me that it was our Lady of Dolours [Sorrows]. Our Lord appeared to bless the world in the same manner as St. Joseph had done. This apparition also vanished and I saw Our Lady once more, this time resembling our Lady of Carmel.[14]

The private visions that the children observed happened in rapid succession. Each time the Blessed Mother had appeared to the children above the holm oak tree in previous apparitions, she was clothed in white. Yet, during these visions, she was wearing a blue mantle and was with St. Joseph and the Christ Child. St. Joseph and the Christ Child were robed in red. St. Joseph imparted the Sign of the Cross above the people three times. As he faded away, Christ appeared at the base of the sun cloaked in red and with his Mother, who was dressed as Our Lady of Sorrows but without the traditional sword through her heart. Christ then gave blessings. When the vision vanished, Lucia received her own private vision of Our Lady of Mount Carmel. This last vision is significant because Lucia later became a Sister of Mount Carmel after a time of being a Dorothean Sister.

The Blessed Mother was faithful to her earlier promises on October 13, 1917. Not only did she reveal her true identity, but she performed a miracle so that the people would believe. She also requested a chapel be built in her honor and asked that the people stop offending God. If anyone present had doubted the children before, surely their hearts were filled with awe and wonder that day!

A Time to Reflect

When Lucia asked the Blessed Mother if she would cure certain people, the Blessed Mother told Lucia, "Some yes, but not others. They must amend their lives and ask forgiveness for their sins."

Another time Our Lady appeared very sad and said, "Do not offend the Lord our God any more, because he is already so much offended."

We all have a grave responsibility to amend our lives and ask forgiveness for our shortcomings and sins. Additionally, we cannot simply be concerned about our own welfare, cures we think we need, and whatever else we desire. God calls us to be generous, selfless, and giving with our time and prayers so that the countless people who are suffering heartache and pain or are steeped in sin (or both) can receive Christ's love through us.

In My Own Life

Can you ponder ways to carve out more time for prayer each day? Do you say a Morning Offering? The Morning Offering is an important prayer in which we hand the reins to God and trust him with our lives. We also ask him to sanctify our prayers and activities, uniting them to his Passion so that they can be transformed and helpful to our own souls and the souls of those we serve. You will find a Morning Offering prayer that you can pray each morning in Appendix A in the "Prayers" section.

Prayer

Dear Lord Jesus and Blessed Mother Mary, help me to be more generous with my prayers and sacrifices for others. Dear St. Joseph, please guide me and help me to help others. Amen.

If desired, you may offer the Morning Offering prayer as well. See page 158.

Chapter Seven

Francisco and Jacinta Go to Heaven

In the world you will have tribulation, but take heart; I have overcome the world" (John 16:33). The message of Fatima invites us to trust in this promise.[1]

Francisco

After the great Miracle of the Sun, the three visionaries continued to pray their daily rosaries and to offer sacrifices and reparation for sinners and for the world. They remembered, of course, that the Blessed Mother had foretold that Francisco and Jacinta would not live in this world for very long.

A year after the October apparition, a terrible influenza epidemic spread, taking about twenty million lives from all over the world. The influenza struck the Marto family, too. During October 1918, with the exception of Ti Marto, the entire Marto family came down with influenza. Thankfully, Ti Marto, being well, could care for his family. Little Francisco became seriously ill. He suffered terribly, but endured bravely, leaning on his faith. Though he wanted to serve his Lord while he remained on earth, he believed in the Blessed Mother's promise that he would soon be in heaven. But, he did not want to waste one ounce of suffering and offered it lovingly to God.

Before Jacinta became too ill herself, she visited her brother in the hospital and reminded him, "Don't forget to make the offering for sinners."

Francisco, suffering a fierce headache, meekly answered, "Yes. But first I make it to console Our Lord and Our Lady, and then, afterwards, for sinners and the Holy Father."[2]

At this time, the Blessed Mother came to visit Francisco and Jacinta and told them that she would come for Francisco very soon and that Jacinta would go to heaven not too long after. Jacinta told Lucia about the Blessed Mother's appearance and that the Blessed Mother asked her if she would like to stay on earth a while longer to save more souls. Jacinta said yes. Jacinta knew that she would be going to a hospital and would suffer much for the salvation of souls.

As Francisco's fever rose, he realized his time on earth was ending, so he asked his father if he could receive the Lord in Holy Communion before he died. Though he had taken the drink of Precious Blood from the chalice given by the Angel of Peace, Francisco had not yet received his First Holy Communion. Still, the priest was called and heard Francisco's confession, promising to bring the Lord in Holy Communion in the morning. Francisco was wracked with pain but thankful he would receive Jesus in the morning. He continued to offer prayers of reparation from his hospital bed and did his best to get to sleep that night.

The next morning the priest was back as promised. Francisco, though very weak and unable to sit up in bed, received the Host on his tongue and then closed his eyes in prayer, offering himself as a victim of love, consolation, and reparation to God.

Lucia came to visit him. "Good-bye, Francisco!" she said. "If you go to heaven tonight, don't forget me when you get there, do you hear me?"

"No, I won't forget. Be sure of that." Francisco grabbed Lucia's hand.

She started to cry but wanted to help her courageous cousin. "Do you want anything more?"

"No," he whispered.

"Good-bye, then, Francisco! Till we meet in heaven, good-bye!"[3]

On April 4, 1919, Francisco again asked pardon for all of his sins. He was ready to go home to heaven. Jacinta came to visit, and as she approached her brother's bed, she cried. She already could not bear the thought of her beloved brother leaving her. Yet, she knew he would be safe and happy with God in heaven. That promise alone gave her consolation.

"Give my love to Our Lord and Our Lady and tell them I'll suffer as much as they want, to convert sinners and to make up to the Immaculate Heart of Mary," Jacinta told him.

The close-knit family stayed near Francisco in a reverent vigil. At ten o'clock that morning, Francisco died. He was ten years old. After Francisco's funeral Mass, his body was buried in St. Anthony's church cemetery in Fatima. On March 12, 1952, he was transferred to a side chapel in the basilica that had been built at the Cova da Iria.

Jacinta

Jacinta missed her brother. She once burst into tears when talking with Lucia and said, "I'd give anything to see him again!"

Jacinta had agreed to the Blessed Mother to stay longer on earth so that she could help save souls by lovingly offering her suffering. Her heart burned with fervor to save souls. She didn't want anyone to go to that terrible place of hell. In her last days she expressed to her cousin Lucia, "I wish I could put into everybody the fire that I have here in my heart which makes me love the Sacred Heart of Jesus and the Immaculate Heart of Mary so much."[4]

Knowing the Sacred Heart of Jesus and the Immaculate Heart of Mary as she did, Jacinta desired so much to save souls and make up for sacrileges and outrages against the Immaculate Heart of Mary as she learned from the Blessed Mother.

This little visionary always exhibited heroic virtues when dealing with her serious sickness. Consistently, she showed care for others above her own desires. Once, when Francisco was in the hospital and Jacinta was sick at home, Jacinta encouraged Lucia to go and visit Francisco first while she offered up a sacrifice of being alone. In addition to making a sacrifice, perhaps being alone was a preparation for what was to come, as The Blessed Mother had told her that she would suffer and die alone.

Jacinta contracted influenza at the same time as the rest of her family. She first suffered with bronchial pneumonia and then a very painful abscess on her little chest. She was sent to the hospital in Ourem. Jacinta prepared her little heart for the sufferings she would endure, always being mindful of the Blessed Mother's promises, but also of Mary's great need for people to make reparation for sinners. Jacinta told her older cousin Lucia that she planned to offer up her pain and suffering for sinners and for the Holy Father. She knew that the doctors wouldn't help her much because the Blessed Mother had already told her that she would not live long. For almost two months, Jacinta was courageous and prayerful at the hospital and offered every bit of pain and suffering to heaven. Her biggest pain was that she couldn't be home with her family. Her heart also ached at the loss of her brother. She reminded herself that he was happy in heaven.

Jacinta was finally released from the hospital because there was little else that could be done for her. She was bedridden, feverish, and had a large open wound in her chest. Tuberculosis and pleurisy were eating at her. Though ravaged in pain and sickness, Jacinta remained passionate about her love for Jesus and Mary, and for saving souls. She reminded Lucia, "We must make many sacrifices and pray a lot for sinners so that no one shall ever again have to go to that prison of fire where people suffer so much."[5]

The beautiful Mother came down again from heaven to console and instruct little Jacinta. The Blessed Mother told Jacinta that she wanted her to go to another hospital in Lisbon. Jacinta immediately and eagerly shared the message with Lucia, saying, "[Our Lady] told me that I'm going to Lisbon, to another hospital, that I will not see you again, nor my parents either, and after suffering a great deal, I shall die alone. But she said I must not be afraid, since she herself is coming to take me to heaven."[6]

Before going to the Lisbon hospital, Jacinta asked her mother to take her one more time to the Cova da Iria and then to say good-bye to Lucia. It was a tough farewell for the girls because they, along with Francisco, were united in an important heavenly mission. Hugging her cousin good-bye tugged fiercely at Lucia's heart and also reminded her that she would soon be the one to stay behind and finish the work.

Jacinta was quick to tell Lucia, "You must stay and tell people that God wants to establish in the world devotion to the Immaculate Heart of Mary." She continued, "When you have to say this, don't hide, but tell everybody that God gives us his grace through the Immaculate Heart of Mary and that people must ask it through her and that the Sacred Heart of Jesus wants the Immaculate Heart of Mary by his side. They must ask peace through the Immaculate Heart because God has given it to her..."[7]

On to the hospital now where Jacinta would finish out her young life with loving prayer. She knew that the hospital stay would not help her health, but she went there out of obedience to heaven's plan. She knew she was to suffer more, but she wouldn't worry or be afraid because Mary promised to come back and bring her to heaven!

When Jacinta was in the Lisbon hospital, she saw the Blessed Mother three more times. The Blessed Mother spoke to Jacinta about penance, about war being a punishment for sin, that certain fashions would be introduced that would offend God, and that more souls go to hell because of sins of the flesh. She also said many marriages were not pleasing to God. The Blessed Mother explained the importance of priests remaining pure and obedient to the Holy Father.[8]

Four days before Jacinta would go home to heaven, the Blessed Mother made a visit to her, bringing her great comfort and assurance. On the evening of February 20, 1920, the Blessed Mother came back to take Jacinta to heaven.

After a funeral Mass, Jacinta was buried in an Ourem cemetery. In 1935, her body was transferred to St. Anthony's parish cemetery in Fatima near her brother Francisco. Jacinta's coffin was exhumed and opened on March 1, 1951, and found to be preserved. She was then placed in a side chapel of the basilica at the Cova da Iria.

On May 13, 2000, the brother and sister Fatima visionaries were beatified by Pope John Paul II at a Solemn Mass in the shrine of the Cova da Iria. Sister Lucia, then a Carmelite nun in Coimbra, Portugal, attended the beatification Mass for her beloved cousins. It is important to note that Francisco and Jacinta were not beatified because they had seen the Blessed Virgin Mary. They were beatified because they lived lives of heroic virtue. In addition, a miracle attributed to their intercession was required before the beautification could take place.

A Time to Reflect

Little Jacinta and Francisco were raised to the altar at their beatification. We know that they were privileged to receive heavenly visits. Let us reflect upon the weight of their responsibility entrusted by heaven. Yes, they received graces to remain faithful to their commitments. But, these children chose to remain faithful. They did not turn their backs or run away. They took on extra suffering so that they could help save souls (wearing the cords under their clothes, not drinking water in the blazing summer heat, choosing to be boiled in oil rather than divulge the Blessed Mother's secrets, Jacinta choosing to stay longer from heaven to save more souls, and more). These children were not beatified because of the heavenly visits, but because Francisco and Jacinta chose to live lives of deep heroic virtue. Theirs is an example for us all.

In My Own Life

Have you been called to give more of your time, talents, or prayer? Do you offer sacrifices for sinners? If not, why? The Blessed Mother calls us all to sacrifice for those in need. We can pray for the graces to be more generous. We can be mindful that God will ask us when we meet him why we were not generous. As Sister Lucia said to her mother in a letter, "Later on we will have eternity for enjoyment. Then, up in Heaven, all that we have suffered will appear nothing; and if we could be sorry, it would be at not having suffered more for the love of Our Lord."[9]

Prayer

Dear Lord Jesus, help me to be more courageous in my daily life. Help me to be more generous in helping others. Blessed Mother Mary, please grant me the graces I need and pray for me. St. Joseph, and all of the angels and saints, please pray for me. Amen.

Chapter Eight

Lucia's Religious Life and the Apparitions at Pontevedra and Tuy, Spain

Here I am, the servant of the Lord.

—Luke 1:38

With Francisco and Jacinta now at their eternal reward, Lucia was left behind to finish the great work of Our Lady's messages at Fatima. She was young, but so very determined to continue to live her life according to God's holy will. At times though, she felt alone. She clung to the comforting promises of the Blessed Mother. Lucia would need to put one foot in front of the other to walk in faith—every day. As a child, she sometimes thought about entering religious life.

The Blessed Mother told Lucia that she was to learn to read and write, so after the death of her cousins, she focused on achieving this goal. She was a smart girl who possessed a good memory and learned well at the local school. But, no matter where Lucia went, she was constantly bombarded with questions and requests. Whether she liked it or not, she was the famous visionary who had communicated with the Queen of Heaven, and those around her were curious and eager to know about her experience.

A new bishop named Dom Jose Alves Correia da Silva came to the diocese of Leiria and was immediately concerned for the humble visionary. He wanted her to learn without the constant badgering. Bishop Correia da Silva made arrangements for Lucia to be taken to the Sisters of Saint Dorothy where she could receive a good and holy education. On June 17, 1921, Lucia entered the college of Dorothean Sisters. There she learned well and also helped with domestic work.

Though she missed her family at home, Lucia was now more prepared to carry out the mission entrusted to her by the Blessed Mother.

Lucia had often felt drawn to a contemplative life as a Carmelite nun. Though she heard the calling to religious life, she believed that she should be grateful to the Dorothean Sisters for the education that she received from them. In 1925, when Lucia was eighteen years old, she entered the Dorothean convent. Certain unrests prevailed in Portugal, due to the anti-clerical attitudes, so the Dorotheans sent their young candidates who were in formation to convents in Spain. Lucia was first in Pontevedra, Spain, and later went to the novitiate house in Tuy, Spain. She professed her final vows in 1934 and became known as Sister Lucia. She remained until 1946. She then went to the Cova da Iria for a few days because she was asked to identify the exact location of the apparitions. Sister Lucia then went to the Dorothean convent near Porto.

On March 25, 1948, Sister Lucia finally embraced the life of prayer that she had earlier desired in being a Carmelite nun. Pope Pius XII granted her permission to transfer to the cloistered Discalced Carmelite Convent in Coimbra, Portugal. She continued to work at saving souls from within the enclosed walls of Carmel of St. Teresa. Her new professed name became Sister Maria Lucia of the Immaculate Heart. Sister Maria Lucia remained there for more than fifty years. She had occasion to leave the cloister when two popes visited the Fatima shrine.

On May 13, 1967, Pope Paul VI invited Sister Maria Lucia to be with him at the Cova da Iria. It was the Golden Jubilee celebration of Our Lady of Fatima's apparitions. When Pope John Paul II visited Fatima on May 13, 1982, to thank the Blessed Mother for sparing his life, and later on May 13, 2000, to beatify Francisco and Jacinta Marto, Sister Maria Lucia was present. What joy this Carmelite must have felt in her heart on all of those occasions, especially on her cousins' beatification day!

As a religious nun, Sister Lucia always strove for perfection in the spiritual life. Just because she had been privileged to see the Blessed Virgin Mary on so many occasions and because she was entrusted with such a great mission did not mean that perfection in her spiritual life was easy. Like all of us, she needed to be burnished in the fire of God's love to grow closer to him. She continued to walk in faith every day, very concerned about perfection in God's eyes, and always cognizant of her faults. Sister Lucia was thankful that one of her confessors ended every one of her confessions with an instruction: "Don't be over-worried by the imperfections of each moment, from which you will be free only in Heaven. With peace and joy, trouble yourself only in increasing the love of God within you."[1]

Sister Lucia suffered much as a religious due to many misunderstandings, mortifications, being questioned about the apparitions, suffering illness, and bearing the tremendous weight of responsibility for all she had experienced. She continued to offer all of her sufferings for the salvation of souls and to seek prayers and counsel from her superiors because she did not want to displease God. In one letter to her spiritual director she said, "I am happy to see that He is not forgetting to purify me and immolate me in the melting pot of suffering. They are relatively small things, but it is His wish that I suffer quite a lot with them."[2]

Fr. Robert J. Fox, a Fatima expert and author of *The Intimate Life of Sister Lucia*, said, "Let us not think, however, that the saints become insensitive. They suffer like anyone else. And like anyone else they have their own particularly sensitive areas." Fr. Fox explained that in one of Sister Lucia's letters "she affirms that the suffering caused by corporal sacrifices was much less than that caused by her having to reveal the communications she received from Our Lord. For this reason she offered herself to God as a victim."[3]

Because Sister Lucia knew the value of offering sufferings to God for the salvation of souls, she discussed with her spiritual director the possibility of offering herself as a victim of love and expiation to God, particularly for Portugal. Jesus, through mystical communion with Sister Lucia during Adoration of the Blessed Sacrament and prayer, revealed to her that Portugal would have to suffer "in consequences of foreign wars."[4]

She wrote to her director, "The motive that inspired me to ask to make this offering was the desire to placate the Divine Justice so unhappy over the sinful lives that the majority of the people of Portugal and all over Europe lead; and to see if, instead of the chastisement that the people are provoking with their ungrateful response to so many graces, they obtain the graces of Peace and Mercy from the Divine Justice."[5]

Sister Lucia feared two things with regard to offering herself fully as a victim. She said she felt "a kind of terror" of diabolical possession that might happen once she made the offering, or that she could possibly lose her mind. She had seen the devil and hell during the July 1917 vision and did not want to see the devil again for fear she would die of fright. Sister Lucia openly discussed these fears with her spiritual director. Her director reminded her, "God doesn't forget those who forget themselves for love of Him."[6] Even with these fears, Sister Lucia set a date for her offering: February 17, 1942—Carnival Day—because she said it was a day "when the World distances itself so much from God."[7]

Regarding her offering herself as a victim, Sister Lucia wrote candidly in another letter, "I asked to be let offer as a victim, promising not to resist Him anymore, offering myself for anything that He wished to ask of me for the salvation of souls. And afterwards, how often have I sought to escape!"[8] Though she wrote that she "sought to escape" her promise to remain a victim for whatever God wanted of her, Sister Lucia was always true to her vows and promises. Her heart deeply desired to save souls and to please God. Every day provided her countless opportunities for offerings, sacrifices, and grace within the details of the day.

When Sister Lucia entered Carmel, she couldn't help but notice the unique cross on the wall of her new cell. After leading her into the small room, the Reverend Mother Prioress asked Sister Lucia about the empty cross, but answered her own question before Sister Lucia could say anything. In 1954, Sister Lucia recounted the conversation and experience when she wrote:

> When I had the good fortune of entering the Carmelite Order, I was led to the cell, and as I was entering it I fixed my eyes on the big stripped cross that opened its arms to me. Our Reverend Mother Prioress asked me: "Do you know why this cross has no statue [corpus]?" And without giving me time to answer she added: "It is so that you may crucify yourself on it." What a beautiful ideal to be crucified with Christ! That He may inebriate me with gladness of the cross. Here lies the secret of my happiness— not to want or wish for more than to love and suffer for love...[9]

On December 29, 1955, Sister Maria Lucia wrote to her Father Superior:

> Difficulties grow everywhere and that is why we need the help of divine grace in order to obtain something that is good. May Our Lady as a loving mother watch over us and help us all. The multitude of letters that arrive here from all over the world bears witness to this. They do little more than complain about the miseries that flood mankind. In view of this I become convinced

that only myself and the little group, who as myself had the good fortune of consecrating themselves to Our Lord, are the only happy people on earth. It is not that one does not live without a Cross, because this is part of being the chosen people. But if it is carried with love, it becomes a treasure of appreciable value, which in fact none of those who follow Christ wants to love.

I don't know if you have ever seen the cell of a Carmelite. In each cell there is a wooden cross without the statue. It is so that following the example of Jesus she should be crucified on it, in order to follow Him step by step to Calvary, where she must suffer and die with Him for love and for the souls that He may want to save through her. Looking this way at the cross, it becomes light and easy to carry; one loves because in it one finds knowledge of union with our God crucified for us, and one does not wish anything more than to love and suffer for love…[10]

The Demanding Path of Perfection

Sister Maria Lucia's life was a continual sacrifice and suffering, but all the while possessing an inner joy and peace in believing in God's promises. She surrendered her heart and strove to become crucified along with her Lord. So many times Sister Maria Lucia was misunderstood or criticized by one Sister or another. It often seemed like she couldn't do anything right. Add to that, Sister Lucia's own critical opinion of her spiritual life, often admitting to have failed over and again. She would say that the state of her soul was "awful." She was so concerned about saving sinners that when she believed she had failed in the spiritual life, she lamented that she was displeasing to Our Lord and wondered how many souls could have been saved had she not acted in a certain way. But, Sister Lucia always picked herself up, dusted herself off, and moved forward in love.

God often leads his children on demanding paths to perfection. At one point Sister Lucia wrote, "I no longer ask for further suffering." She desired only "what His Divine Mercy deigns to send me."[11] She lived in accordance with the words of the Angel of Peace: "Make of everything you can a sacrifice, and offer it to God, as an act of reparation for the sins by which He is offended, and in supplication for the conversion of sinners. You will draw down peace upon your country.... Above all, accept and bear with submission the suffering which the Lord will send you."

Sister Maria Lucia had a big heart, spending her time in prayer and service to others. As a Carmelite nun she made rosaries and wrote countless letters of spiritual direction and encouragement to seminarians. Many people wrote to Sister Lucia over the years, and she answered their numerous letters even though she was very limited with regard to visitors.

Sister Maria Lucia asked permission from her Mother Superior to rise earlier than the rest of the Community to ring the rising bell and pray certain prayers with arms outstretched early in the morning, as well as to stay in the chapel later than everyone else on certain nights.

Sister Maria Lucia explained these things in a letter to her Father Superior: "My most sincere wish to love Him and to prove my love for Him, above all in sacrifice, is at all times directed to Him alone." She briefly mentioned some of her sacrifices to keep the Father up to date. She then wrote, "It seems to me that I am practicing an act of charity on the Sr. who had this [bell-ringing] function, and give Our Lord one more proof of love. It is a small thing, but He knows I am not capable of great things; and I believe it is one more way of expelling the spirit of self-indulgence at night and uniting myself to the Good Lord who prayed so often at night, and how often would He not do it for me?"[12]

Sister Maria Lucia understood the value of redemptive suffering and of making sacrifices for the Lord. Once she told her sick mother, who was extremely sad at not being able to see her daughter, that it was a suffering that the Lord requested.

She explained in a letter that she understood her mother's pain. "The sacrifice of not being able to embrace all your children gives you as much, if not more, suffering as corporal pain would; but this sacrifice is being asked of us by Him Who has the right to ask and Who also first, for love of us, was separated from His Most Holy Mother, in a much more sorrowful manner, namely by death on a cross," she wrote. For the love of saving souls, Sister Lucia was even willing to give up seeing her own mother before she left this earth. "This life is for suffering," Sister Lucia told her. "Later on we will have eternity for enjoyment. Then, up in Heaven, all that we have suffered will appear nothing; and if we could be sorry, it would be at not having suffered more for the love of Our Lord."[13]

Sister Maria Lucia pressed on with her commitment to spread devotion to the Immaculate Heart of Mary and to convince the pope and bishops of the world to consecrate Russia to the Immaculate Heart of Mary. She also knew she needed to spread the devotion of the Five First Saturdays. The Blessed Mother's requests were constantly on Sister Maria Lucia's mind. As well, were her admonitions, "Many souls are going to Hell for the want of someone to make sacrifices and pray for them." Her holy Mother's words prodded her to continue to make every moment count. Sister Maria Lucia immersed herself in prayer and generous sacrifices for the glory of God.

Sister Maria Lucia—who was sometimes still referred to as, and even often signed her name simply as, "Sister Lucia"—remained a nun in the Carmelite convent until her death on February 13, 2005. When the Blessed Mother told Lucia that she was taking Francisco and Jacinta to heaven, she'd said, "But you are to stay here some time longer. Jesus wishes to make use of you to make me known and loved. He wants to establish in the world devotion to my Immaculate Heart." That "some time longer" turned out to be eighty-eight more years!

But let us now look at the next apparitions of the Blessed Virgin Mary to Sister Maria Lucia.

The First Apparition at Pontevedra, Spain: December 10, 1925

Sister Lucia was a postulant in the Congregation of the Dorothean Sisters in Pontevedra, Spain, when the Blessed Mother came to visit her again. The Blessed Mother requested something called the "Communion of Reparation" in three apparitions. Sister Lucia's spiritual director at the time, Fr. P. Aparicio, SJ, requested that she write down the apparitions, but in the third person.

Sister Lucia describes the first apparition at Pontevedra, Spain:

> On December 10, 1925, the most holy Virgin appeared to her, and by her side, elevated on a luminous cloud, was [the Christ] child. The most holy Virgin rested her hand on [Sister Lucia's] shoulder, and as she did so, she showed her a heart encircled in thorns, which she was holding in her other hand. At the same time, the [Christ] Child said: "Have compassion on the Heart of your most holy Mother, covered with thorns, with which ungrateful men pierce it at every moment, and there is no one to make an act of reparation to remove them." Then the most holy Virgin said: "Look, my daughter, at my Heart, surrounded with thorns with which ungrateful men pierce me at every moment by their blasphemies and ingratitude. You at least try to console me and say that I promise to assist at the hour of death, with the graces necessary for salvation, all those who, on the first Saturday of five consecutive months, shall confess [their sins], receive Holy Communion, recite five decades of the rosary, and keeping me

company for fifteen minutes while meditating on the fifteen mysteries of the rosary, with the intention of making reparation to me."[14]

This was not the first time that Sister Lucia saw the Sorrowful Heart of Mary. During the June 13, 1917, apparition, she and her two cousins saw a similar crown of thorns encircling a heart when the Blessed Mother opened her hands to the great light. The crown of thorns piercing her heart symbolized the sins that offended the Blessed Mother. When Lucia wrote about the image of the apparition at the Cova da Iria that occurred on June 13, she said, "We understood that this was the Immaculate Heart of Mary, outraged by the sins of humanity, and seeking reparation."[15]

Now in this new apparition, Sister Lucia sees the Christ Child who is begging compassion on holy Mother Mary because of the terrible, painful thorns inflicted by ungrateful men who "pierce it at every moment." Further, he is grieved that there is no one that will make an act of reparation to remove the thorns.

The Blessed Mother also begs help when she asks Sister Lucia to try to console her. She then promises the graces necessary for salvation. What a promise! The Blessed Mother tells Sister Lucia about the Five First Saturdays devotion. Some experts say that the Five First Saturdays devotion might be the most neglected devotion of Fatima. Many have focused more on the consecration of Russia than on their own part of partaking in the devotion to save souls. Fr. Andrew Apostoli, CFR, wrote:

> Many people have unfortunately put such stress on the consecration of Russia by the Holy Father as the condition for the triumph of the Immaculate Heart of Mary and peace in the world, that they have forgotten or neglected the fact that our Lady also asked for the Five First Saturdays devotion.... Pope

John Paul II has done his part in making the consecration of Russia to the Immaculate Heart, but are we, as Mary's children, doing our part by devotion to first Saturdays?[16]

The Blessed Mother teaches us that there are four main parts and two conditions to the Five First Saturdays devotion. The four parts are: (1) go to the sacrament of confession on the First Saturday or during the week before or after it, (2) receive Holy Communion, (3) recite five decades of the rosary, and (4) keep Our Lady company for fifteen minutes by meditating on the mysteries of the rosary.

The two conditions necessary for this devotion are that the practices be done on the first Saturday of five consecutive months, and that they be done with the intention of making reparation to Our Lady for the sins of ingratitude and blasphemy committed against her. The Five First Saturdays devotion will be discussed in greater depth in a following chapter.

The Second Apparition at Pontevedra, Spain: February 15, 1926

The second apparition at Pontevedra was an interesting one. In this apparition, the Christ Child surprised Lucia when he appeared to her. She did not recognize him at first. During the last apparition, which occurred a little over two months prior, the Blessed Mother appealed to Sister Lucia to spread the devotion of the Five First Saturdays. Sister Lucia's confessor did not propagate the devotion. He wanted further happenings to prove the credibility and necessity of the devotion. The hands of Sister Lucia's mother superior were tied because of the confessor's stand on the matter. Sister Lucia explained:

> On the 15th (of February 1926), I was very busy at my work, and was not thinking of [the devotion] at all. I went to throw out a pan full of rubbish beyond the vegetable garden, in the same place where, some months earlier, I had met a child. I had asked him if he knew the Hail Mary, and he said he did, whereupon I

requested him to say it so I could hear him. But, as he made no attempt to say it himself, I said it with him three times over, at the end of which I asked him to say it alone. But as he remained silent and was unable to say the Hail Mary alone, I asked him if he knew where the Church of Santa Maria was, to which he replied that he did. I had him go there every day to say this [prayer]: "O, my heavenly Mother, give me your Child Jesus!" I taught him this, and then left him…. Going there as usual, I found a child who seemed to me to be the same one whom I had previously met, so I questioned him: "Did you ask our heavenly Mother for the Child Jesus?" The child turned to me and said: "And have you spread through the world what our heavenly Mother requested of you?" With that, he was transformed into the resplendent Child. Knowing then that it was Jesus, I said: "My Jesus, you know very well what my confessor said to me in the letter I read to You. He told me that it was necessary for this vision to be repeated, for further happenings to prove its credibility, and he added that Mother Superior, on her own, could do nothing to propagate this devotion."[17]

Sister Lucia was deeply grateful for the visit from the Christ Child. However, she found herself in a tough situation because the people to whom she owed obedience were not helping to spread the devotion. Jesus himself was there to ask why she hadn't spread the devotion. She was not sure what more she could possibly do except to pray. Sister Lucia's confessor had even questioned why the devotion would be necessary, arguing that some people already observed a devotion to praying the rosary on the First Saturdays and were already receiving Holy Communion. Sister Lucia communicated that to the Christ Child. He said:

It is true, my daughter, that many souls begin the First Saturdays, but few finish them, and those who do complete them do so in order to receive the graces that are promised thereby. It would please me more if they did Five with fervor and with the intention of making reparation to the Heart of your heavenly Mother, than if they did Fifteen in a tepid and indifferent manner.[18]

Sister Lucia's Mother Superior was ready to spread the devotion but had been discouraged because the confessor said that alone she could do nothing. So, she waited. The Christ Child reassured Sister Lucia:

It is true your Superior alone can do nothing, but with my grace she can do all. It is enough that your confessor gives you permission and that your Superior speaks of it, for it to be believed, even without people knowing to whom it has been revealed.[19]

We can indeed take our Lord's words to our own hearts. He tells us that, with his grace, all things can be done according to God's holy will.

The Third Apparition at Pontevedra, Spain: December 17, 1927

Since the second apparition, Sister Lucia had been very busy with her duties and her deep prayers. She was always concerned about pleasing the Lord, growing in holiness, and fulfilling her duties well. Now a novice, not quite two years later, Sister Lucia asked the Lord a specific question when praying before him in the tabernacle in the chapel at Pontevedra. She desperately wanted an answer. How could she answer her superiors about the origin of the devotion to the Immaculate Heart of Mary without revealing the secret Our Lady told her to keep in the utmost confidence? How much could she talk about? Was she allowed to speak of any of it to her superiors? Jesus told her:

My daughter, write what they ask of you. Write also all that the most holy Virgin revealed to you in the Apparition [July 13], in which she spoke of this devotion. As for the remainder of the

Secret, continue to keep silence.[20]

Sister Lucia now knew that she could reveal the First and Second Secret but must still keep the Third Secret confidential.

Revelation from Jesus in Tuy, Spain: May 29–30, 1930

Sister Lucia was transferred to a convent in Tuy, Spain. She continued her duties there and prayed continuously, still being questioned by various people about the importance of the Five First Saturdays devotion. Sister Lucia's confessor in Tuy, Fr. Jose Bernardo Goncalves, SJ, asked why the devotion is specifically for *five* Saturdays. Sister Lucia wrote a letter to him on June 12, 1930, and described her encounter and conversation with the Lord in the chapel:

> Remaining in the chapel with our Lord, part of the night of the 29th-30th of that month of May 1930, talking to our Lord about [some of those] questions, I suddenly felt possessed more intimately by the Divine Presence; and if I am not mistaken, the following was revealed to me: "Daughter, the motive is simple. There are five kinds of offenses and blasphemies spoken against the Immaculate Heart of Mary: blasphemies (1) against her Immaculate Conception; (2) against her perpetual virginity; (3) against her divine maternity, refusing at the same time to accept her as the Mother of mankind; (4) by those who try publicly to implant in the hearts of children an indifference, contempt, and even hate for this Immaculate Mother; and (5) for those who insult her directly in her sacred images.[21]

Jesus also told Sister Lucia that his own Mother, in wanting to save her beloved children from hell, had asked for these acts of reparation so that Jesus would be moved to forgive those souls who had offended her. Jesus then asked Sister Lucia to do her part: "As for you, try incessantly with your prayers and sacrifices to move me into mercifulness towards those poor souls." How could she not be moved and more committed to make additional sacrifices? Our Lord himself had asked it of her. He asks it of all of us as well.

Jesus then spoke about the carrying out of the Five First Saturdays devotion. He said those who could not carry out the requirement on the First Saturday would be allowed to do so on the Sunday (the day after), if their priests were willing to make allowances for just reasons. The allowance was very beneficial to those traveling long distances to church and when it was difficult to do so two days in a row—for confession and Holy Communion and back on Sunday for Mass.

The Apparition at Tuy, Spain: June 13, 1929

Sister Lucia remained in Tuy, Spain, until she made her perpetual profession of vows of the Sisters of Saint Dorothy on October 3, 1934. While she was in the Tuy convent, the Blessed Mother came to tell her that it was time for the pope to consecrate Russia to her Immaculate Heart. But as we will see later, this would not happen until 1984 when Pope John Paul II made the consecration.

Sister Lucia had been trying very hard with her superiors and confessors to promote the messages entrusted to her. She did not let one opportunity pass without trying to get official approval. But, so far it was to no avail. Then, on the evening of June 13, 1929, alone in the chapel, Sister Lucia received a new mystical amazing grace in a vision of the Most Holy Trinity. Sister Lucia was making a holy hour of Eucharistic Adoration when she saw something quite extraordinary. She described it thus:

> I had sought and obtained permission of my Superiors and Confessor to make a Holy Hour from eleven o'clock until midnight, every Thursday to Friday night. Being alone one night, I knelt near the altar rails in the middle of the chapel and, prostrate, I prayed the prayers of the Angel. Feeling tired, I then stood

up and continued to pray with my arms in the form of a cross. The only light was that of the sanctuary lamp. Suddenly the whole chapel was illuminated by a supernatural light, and above the altar appeared a cross of light reaching to the ceiling

In a brighter light, on the upper part of the cross, could be seen the face of a man and his body as far as the waist; Upon his breast was a dove of light; nailed to the cross, the body of another man. A little below the waist, I could see a chalice and a large host suspended in the air, on to which some drops of blood were falling from the face of Jesus Crucified and from a wound in His side. These drops ran down on to the host and fell into the chalice.

Beneath the right arm of the cross, was Our Lady and in her hand was her Immaculate Heart. (It was Our Lady of Fatima with her Immaculate Heart in her left hand, without sword or roses, but with a crown of thorns and flames.) Under the left arm of the cross, large letters, as if of crystal clear water which ran upon the altar, formed these words: "Grace and Mercy." I understood that it was the Mystery of the Holy Trinity which was shown to me, and I received lights about this mystery which I am not permitted to reveal.[22]

We can only imagine the sheer beauty of this vision. It is rich in meaning. Fr. Andrew Apostoli, CFR, compares the vision of the Most Holy Trinity to what happens at the Consecration at the Holy Sacrifice of the Mass. He wrote:

At the Consecration, God the Father receives Jesus, who renews the offering himself that he made on the Cross as the Victim for our sins. Then in turn the Father gives Christ in the Eucharist to us as the Bread of Life. The Holy Spirit is present, invoked by the priest to come and sanctify the gifts of bread and wine by transforming them into the very Body, Blood, Soul, and Divinity of

Jesus Christ. The bread and wine are consecrated separately to signify Christ's death, for a person dies when his blood is separated from his body; thus, the death of Jesus on the Cross is sacramentally renewed in every Mass.[23]

What about the Blessed Mother? How does she fit into this vision? Sister Lucia described the Blessed Mother as Our Lady of Fatima holding her heart with a crown of thorns and flames in her left hand. We recall words from Scripture when Mary was given to mankind by her Son Jesus, "Then he said to the disciple, 'Here is your mother.' And from that hour the disciple took her into his own home" (John 19:27).

When considering Mary's role in salvation history and her representation in the vision, we can look back in time to the prophecy of Simeon: "Then Simeon blessed them and said to his mother Mary, 'This child is destined for the falling and the rising of many in Israel, and to be a sign that will be opposed so that the inner thoughts of many will be revealed—and a sword will pierce your own soul too' (Luke 2:34–35).

Fr. Apostoli explained, "Our Lady is present in the vision because she was at the foot of the Cross on Calvary. For this reason, Saint Padre Pio used to say, 'When you go to the Holy Sacrifice of the Mass, picture yourself standing below the Cross of Jesus, next to His Blessed Mother, next to Saint John the Beloved Disciple, and next to Saint Mary Magdalene, for in spirit that is where you are!'"[24]

The Blessed Mother is shown with her Sorrowful Heart. We can certainly bear in mind that our Mother in Heaven is always joined to her Son Jesus's sufferings on the cross. Our loving Mother offers her sufferings to our heavenly Father begging reparation for the sins of the world and for the salvation of souls.

Mary's place in God's plan is higher than of any other person. The

Blessed Mother's Immaculate Heart should be a part of our lives. Mary's Immaculate Heart is a central part of the message of Fatima. The Cross of Jesus is central to our faith as Catholics. Let us for a moment reflect upon St. Louis de Montfort's words:

> By His death, the ignominies of the Cross were made so glorious, its poverty and bareness so opulent, its pains so sweet, its hardness so attractive, that it became as it were deified and an object of adoration for angels and men. Jesus now demands that, with Him, all His subjects adore it.... On the day of the last judgment He will...command the chief Seraphim and Cherubim to gather up throughout the whole world all the particles of the true Cross, and they will be so well reunited by His loving omnipotence that they will form but one Cross, the very Cross upon which He died. He will have His Cross borne in triumph by the angels who will sing its joyful praises. His Cross will go before Him placed upon the most brilliant cloud that ever appeared. He will judge the world with His Cross and by it. What will be the joy of the friends of the Cross on beholding it? What will be the despair of its enemies, who not being able to bear the brilliant sight of this Cross will cry out to the mountains to fall upon them, and to the depths of hell to swallow them up!

Pondering this vision, we can reflect on the Precious Blood of Jesus coming from the wounds on his sacred head made by the crown of thorns and from his pierced side. The Precious Blood falls onto the Host and is caught in the chalice, which is suspended in the air under the Host. We can contemplate that the Body and Blood of Jesus that we partake in the Eucharist is truly the Body and Blood of Christ— it is the same as the Blood that is falling into the chalice in this vision. We learn the value of Jesus's suffering and death from St. Peter who said, "You know that you were ransomed from the futile ways inherited from your ancestors, not with perishable things like silver or gold, but with the precious blood of Christ, like that of a lamb without defect or blemish" (1 Peter 1:18-19). Jesus's Precious Blood is the cost of our redemption.

The words "grace" and "mercy" give us much to think about. Sister Lucia described the words "as if of crystal clear water which ran upon the altar." Water is very significant to our faith. There is the baptismal element, and of course, there is the living water significance we recall spoken by Jesus to the Samaritan woman: "The water that I will give will become in them a spring of water gushing up to eternal life." (John 4:14). Grace and mercy are the fruits of Jesus's Passion and death on the Cross, which flow through the Holy Sacrifice of the Mass.

Finally, Sister Lucia states that she was given "lights" to understand the mystery of the Holy Trinity which was shown to her in the vision.

The Blessed Mother Speaks to Sister Lucia about the Consecration

Sister Lucia observed the great vision in the chapel and took the "lights" she received to her heart. Then the Blessed Mother spoke to her:

> The moment has come in which God asks the Holy Father, in union with all the Bishops of the world, to make the consecration of Russia to my Immaculate Heart, promising to save it by this means. There are so many souls whom the Justice of God condemns for sins committed against me, that I have come to ask reparation: sacrifice yourself for this intention and pray.[25]

Almost twelve years prior, the Blessed Mother had told Sister Lucia and her two younger cousins that she would return to request the consecration of Russia to her Immaculate Heart. She foretold another horrific war which would break out during Pope Pius XI's pontificate if the people did not heed her warning and stop offending God. There would be a great sign in the sky that would appear before the war. Indeed, in 1938 a great, colorful sky like a brilliant aurora borealis was sighted all over Europe and parts of the United States.

A Time to Reflect

We might think that our spiritual lives are going to be smooth and easy. But God often leads his children on demanding paths to perfection. Even as a child, Lucia took on many sacrifices and penances to help save souls. At one point in religious life, Sister Lucia wrote, "I no longer ask for further suffering." This was because she desired only "what His Divine Mercy deigns to send me."

The Angel of Peace's words to the three young shepherd children, which remained in Sister Lucia's heart were: "Make of everything you can a sacrifice, and offer it to God, as an act of reparation for the sins by which He is offended, and in supplication for the conversion of sinners. You will draw down peace upon your country.... Above all, accept and bear with submission, the suffering which the Lord will send you."

In My Own Life

Our Lady of Fatima calls us to make sacrifices and do penances so that we can help to save souls. But let's not forget to offer up our daily duties. Remember, the Angel of Peace told the children, "Offer up everything in your power as a sacrifice to the Lord in reparation for the sins by which He is offended, and in supplication for the conversion of sinners.... More than all else, accept and bear with resignation the sufferings that God may send you." Remember to start every day with a Morning Offering so that your prayers, works, joys, and sufferings can be redeemed by Jesus and transformed to help your soul and the souls of others you serve. Try your best to offer up all of your inconveniences, sorrows, and pain to God, asking for the grace you need, that all of it can be used for the good.

Can you make the commitment to make the Five First Saturdays? Even if you have done so in the past, countless graces await you in the next Five First Saturdays. As well, countless souls can be saved by your small sacrifice. The Blessed Mother even guarantees to assist us at the hour of our deaths. Why are we not embracing this First Saturday devotion? But, let's do it out of love for Our Lord, Our Lady, and to help save souls.

Prayer

Dear Lord Jesus, I pray to offer my life to you—every single moment, every breath I take. Our Lady of Fatima, please grant me the graces to be a generous soul for the salvation of souls. St. Joseph, and all of the angels and saints, please pray for me. Amen.

Chapter Nine

THE CONSECRATION OF RUSSIA TO THE IMMACULATE HEART OF MARY

Tell everyone that God gives us His grace through His Mother's Immaculate Heart, which He wants to hold close to His own Sacred Heart. The people must ask for peace through Mary's Immaculate Heart, because that is the way God wants it, and that is what our Lady herself has told us![1]

—Blessed Jacinta to Sister Lucia

The Immaculate Heart of Mary is very much an integral part of the Fatima messages. We know that the Blessed Mother spoke to the children about the importance of devotion to her Immaculate Heart. She also told them that God desired to establish devotion to her Immaculate Heart as a means to save souls from the fate of hell.

On her death bed, Jacinta spoke of this and reminded Lucia of her responsibilities after Jacinta would go to heaven. She said:

I shall go to heaven very soon, Lucia, and you must stay to explain to people how God wants to establish devotion to the Immaculate Heart of Mary all over the world. And when you speak of this to people, Lucia, don't be afraid to tell exactly what is true. Tell everyone that God gives us His grace through His Mother's Immaculate Heart, which He wants to hold close to His own Sacred Heart. The people must ask for peace through Mary's Immaculate Heart, because that is the way God wants it, and that is what our Lady herself has told us![2]

Hope in the Immaculate Heart of Mary

When Pope Emeritus Benedict XVI was Cardinal Ratzinger, he underscored the hope that we have in the Blessed Mother's promise that "my Immaculate Heart will triumph." He wrote:

> I would like finally to mention another key expression of the "secret" which has become justly famous: "my Immaculate Heart will triumph." What does this mean? The Heart open to God, purified by contemplation of God, is stronger than guns and weapons of every kind. The *fiat* of Mary, the word of her heart, has changed the history of the world, because it brought the Savior into the world—because, thanks to her *Yes,* God could become man in our world and remains so for all time. The Evil One has power in this world, as we see and experience continually; he has power because our freedom continually lets itself be led away from God. But since God himself took a human heart and has thus steered human freedom towards what is good, the freedom to choose evil no longer has the last word. From that time forth, the word that prevails is this: "In the world you will have tribulation, but take heart; I have overcome the world" (*John* 16:33). The message of Fatima invites us to trust in this promise."[3]

When Sister Lucia was a Dorothean Sister living in Tuy, Spain, the Blessed Mother appeared to her on June 13, 1929. It was during a Holy Hour of reparation that Sister Lucia was making in the convent chapel shortly before midnight when she was given that stunning vision of the Holy Trinity. We have discussed this already, but for now we touch upon it because the Blessed Mother told Sister Lucia that the time had come for the Holy Father to make the consecration of Russia to her Immaculate Heart.

Support for the Consecration of Russia

During this time, there lived a mystic in the area of Fatima known as Alexandrina da Costa (1904-1955). She lived in Balasar, which is north of Fatima. Pope John Paul II said this about Alexandrina in his homily at her beatification ceremony on April 25, 2004:

"Do you love me?"Jesus asks Simon Peter, who replies: "Yes Lord, you know that I love you."The life of Blessed Alexandrina Maria da Costa can be summarized in this dialogue of love. Permeated and burning with this anxiety of love, she wished to deny nothing to her Savior. With a strong will, she accepted everything to demonstrate her love for him. A 'spouse of blood', she mystically relived Christ's passion and offered herself as a victim for sinners, receiving strength from the Eucharist: this became her only source of nourishment for the final 13 years of her life. With the example of Blessed Alexandrina, expressed in the trilogy "suffer, love, make reparation," Christians are able to discover the stimulus and motivation to make "noble" all that is painful and sad in life through the greatest evidence of love: sacrificing one's life for the beloved. Secret of holiness: love for Christ."

When Alexandrina was attacked by a man, she tried to preserve her chastity by escaping from him. In the process, she fell out a window and was completely paralyzed. Instead of becoming angry and bitter, she offered her crippling pain along with heartfelt prayers and penances continually to Jesus to make reparation for sinners and for their conversions. She was a chosen soul and was favored by Jesus with being relieved of her paralysis three hours every Friday so that she could mystically experience the sufferings of Jesus's passion. Alexandrina also experienced many attacks from the devil.

Alexandrina was given a revelation from God to ask Pope Pius XI to consecrate the world to the Immaculate Heart of Mary. She made this request through her spiritual director in a 1936 letter to Vatican Secretary of State Cardinal Pacelli (who was later Pope Pius XII). Alexandrina prayed deeply for this request and offered her sufferings.

At that time, the bishops of Portugal made an Ignatian retreat at Fatima and sent a letter of their own to request the consecration of the world to the Immaculate Heart of Mary.

For the last thirteen years of her life, Alexandrina ate no food and was nourished only by Holy Communion. She died on October 13, 1955 (Feast of Our Lady of Fatima). The Holy See investigated Alexandrina's sanctity, and she was beautified in 2004.

Pope Pius XI did not make the consecration that Our Lady of Fatima requested. We may wonder why he did not. He may have ignored any pressure to act on what might be considered a private revelation. But there may also be another reason. Fr. Andrew Apostoli, CFR, points out that during Pius XI's pontificate the pontiff was asked why he treated the saintly Padre Pio severely by placing harsh restrictions upon him. His answer was, "I have not been badly disposed towards Padre Pio, but I have been badly informed."

In *Fatima For Today*, Fr. Andrew Apostoli, CFR, wrote:

There are reliable reports that Communist sympathizers, especially Freemasons, had infiltrated the Vatican around this time. Bella Dodd, an ex-communist who was received into the Church by Bishop Sheen, told him in 1950 that as a Communist in the 1930's she recruited men with no vocations to enter the ranks of the priesthood in order to destroy the Catholic Church from within. This plan, she said, had come directly from Joseph Stalin (a former seminarian…), who was the head of the Communist Party throughout the world at the time. He has said that the Roman Catholic Church was the greatest enemy of Communism and that the way to destroy the Church was to infiltrate the priesthood. Dodd told Bishop Sheen that the Communists had "four contacts" high up in the Vatican. These were believed to be four cardinals who were Freemasons. Bishop Sheen forbade her to reveal their names. Is it possible that Pope Pius XI had been

"badly informed" about Our Lady of Fatima's request to consecrate Russia?"[4]

So we see that there were other pleas for the consecration of the
world to the Immaculate Heart of Mary other than Sister Lucia's
numerous requests. There are the Portuguese bishops and also Blessed
Alexandrina. Though we can never know Pope Pius XI's thoughts,
we know there is the possibility that corruption may have tarnished
the information reaching Pope Pius XI, thus preventing him from
making the consecration.

Pope Pius XII Consecrates the World and Later Russia

In 1940, Sister Lucia wrote another letter to Bishop da Silva of
Leiria. She was saddened that the consecration had not taken place.
She wrote, "Would that the world knew the hour of grace that is
being given it would do penance!"

On December 2, 1940, Sister Lucia wrote a letter directly to Pope
Pius XII (1939–1958) in obedience to her confessor, requesting the
consecration of the world and Russia to the Immaculate Heart. We
can learn a lot from her heartfelt plea to the pontiff. She wrote:

Most Holy Father,

Humbly prostrated at your feet, I come as the last sheep of the
fold entrusted to you to open my heart, by order of my spiritual
director.

I am the only survivor of the children to whom our Lady
appeared in Fatima (Portugal) from the 13th of May to the
13th of October 1917. The Blessed Virgin has granted me many
graces, the greatest of all being my admission to the Institute of
Saint Dorothy....

I come, Most Holy Father, to renew a request that has already
been brought to you several times. The request, Most Holy Father,
is from our Lord and our good Mother in Heaven.

In 1917, in the portion of the apparitions that we have designated "the secret," the Blessed Virgin revealed the end of the war
that was then afflicting Europe, and predicted another forth-
coming, saying that to prevent it She would come and ask the
consecration of Russia to Her Immaculate Heart as well as the
Communion of reparation on the first Saturday. She promised peace and the conversion of that nation if Her request was
attended to. She announced that otherwise this nation would
spread her errors throughout the world, and there would be wars,
persecutions of the Holy Church, martyrdom of many Christians,
several persecutions and sufferings reserved for Your Holiness,
and the annihilation of several nations.

Most Holy Father, this remained a secret until 1926 according
to the express will of our Lady. Then, in a revelation She asked
that the Communion of reparation on the first Saturdays of five
consecutive months be propagated throughout the world, with
its conditions of doing the following with the same purpose:
going to confession, meditating for a quarter of an hour on the
mysteries of the rosary and saying the rosary with the aim of
making reparation for the insults, sacrileges and indifferences
committed against Her Immaculate Heart. Our good Heavenly
Mother promises to assist the persons who practice this devotion,
in the hour of their death, with all the necessary graces for their
salvation. I exposed the request of our Lady to my confessor, who
tried to have it fulfilled, but only on the 13th of September 1939
did His Excellency the Bishop of Leiria make public in Fatima
this request of our Lady.

I take this opportunity, Most Holy Father, to ask you to bless
and extend this devotion to the whole world. In 1929, through
another apparition, our Lady asked for the consecration of Russia
to Her Immaculate Heart, promising its conversion through this

means and the hindering of the propagation of its errors.

Sometime afterwards I told my confessor of the request of our Lady. He tried to fulfill it by making it known to Pius XI.

In several intimate communications our Lord has not stopped insisting on this request, promising lately, to shorten the days of tribulation which He has determined to punish the nations for their crimes, through war, famine and several persecutions of the Holy Church and Your Holiness, if you will consecrate the world to the Immaculate Heart of Mary, with a special mention for Russia, and order that all the Bishops of the world do the same in union with Your Holiness. I truly feel your sufferings, Most Holy Father! And, as much as I can through my humble prayers and sacrifices, I try to lessen them, close to our Lord and the Immaculate Heart of Mary.

Most Holy Father, if in the union of my soul with God I have not been deceived, our Lord promises a special protection to our country in this war, due to the consecration of the nation by the Portuguese Prelates, to the Immaculate Heart of Mary; as proof of the graces that would have been granted to other nations, had they also consecrated themselves to Her.

Now, Most Holy Father, allow me to make one more request, which is but an ardent wish of my humble heart; that the feast in honor of the Immaculate Heart of Mary be extended throughout the whole world as one of the main feasts of the Holy Church.

With the deepest respect and reverence, I ask for the Apostolic Blessing. May God protect Your Holiness.

Tuy, Spain, 2nd of December of 1940.

Maria Lucia de Jesus[5]

Pope Pius XII was consecrated a bishop on May 13, 1917, which was the day of the first Fatima apparition. Pope Pius XII was a deeply Marian pope who on November 1, 1950, solemnly proclaimed the dogma of the Assumption of the Blessed Virgin Mary (that at the end of her life, the Blessed Mother was fully assumed body and soul into heaven). He also proclaimed a Marian Year (December 8, 1953 to December 8, 1954) to celebrate the centenary of the proclamation of the dogma of the Immaculate Conception of Mary, that she was conceived without original sin, filled with a fullness of grace from her Son Jesus. This pope also instituted the Feast of the Queenship of Mary on August 22, as well as a renewal for the consecration of the human race every year to the Immaculate Heart of Mary on this feast day since Mary is Queen of Heaven and Earth.

Pope Pius XII consecrated the world to the Immaculate Heart of Mary at the closing of the Silver Jubilee Year of Fatima on October 31, 1942. He had been urged to do so by the bishops of Portugal, Blessed Alexandrina, and Sister Lucia. He gave a special mention of Russia to the Immaculate Heart of Mary.

Here he gives reference to the world:

> To you, to your Immaculate Heart, We, as universal Father of the great Christian family, as Vicar of Him to Whom has been given all power over Heaven and earth, and from Whom we have received the care of all souls redeemed by His Blood, who inhabit the world; to you, to your Immaculate Heart, in this tragic hour of human history, we entrust, we offer, we consecrate, not only Holy Church, the Mystical Body of your Son Jesus, which suffers and bleeds in so many places and in so many ways, but also the whole world torn by moral strife, ablaze with hate and victim of its own sins.[6]

He gives this reference to Russia:

> Give peace to the peoples separated from us by error or by schism, and especially to those who profess such singular devotion to you and in whose homes as honored place was ever accorded your

venerable icon (today perhaps often kept hidden to await better days); bring them back to the one true fold of Christ under the one shepherd.[7]

Pope Pius XII made this consecration with only the bishops of Portugal gathered in the Cathedral of Lisbon. On the Feast of the Immaculate Conception, six weeks later on December 8, 1942, he repeated the consecration at St. Peter's Basilica in Rome before forty thousand people. There were only a small number of bishops present, yet the Blessed Mother had asked for all of the bishops of the world. Because not all bishops were united in the consecration, it was not effective. Neither of the two consecrations was effective because they did not include all of the bishops of the world.

However, Sister Lucia said Jesus expressed his joy over the consecration to her when he appeared to her in the spring of 1943. Shortly after the consecration, the first significant victory was won for the Allies—Germany lost the Battle of Stalingrad. Even though the German invasion remained committed to Communism, it was the beginning of the end of the Third Reich.

On July 7, 1952, ten years later, Pope Pius XII consecrated the Church and the world, with a special mention of Russia, to the Immaculate Heart of Mary. Pope Pius XII explicitly consecrated the Russian people to the Immaculate Heart of Mary in *Sacro Vergente Anno*, an Apostolic Letter. But because the world's bishops did not participate, it did not fulfill Our Lady of Fatima's requests to convert Russia.

Pope John XXIII

Pope John XXIII did not visit Fatima while he was pope, but he did visit as Cardinal Roncalli on May 13, 1956. He read the Third Secret of Fatima, though he did not attempt a consecration of Russia with the bishops. The Council of Bishops discussed the need to consecrate the world to the Immaculate Heart of Mary, but Russia was not mentioned specifically.

Why was Russia not mentioned, as Our Lady had asked? Pope John XXIII was responsible for convoking the Second Vatican Council and had persuaded Russian Orthodox observers to attend the Council sessions. He had guaranteed there would be no arguments about the Church and the Marxist government. Because of this it is thought that the language of adding Russia to a consecration at that time would not be a good idea.

Pope Paul VI

Pope Paul VI was elected on June 21, 1963, after the death of Pope John XXIII, and took over leadership of the Second Vatican Council. As the third session began, the new pope requested that the Council Fathers put their hope and trust in the Blessed Virgin Mary. And so, on November 21, 1964, the Feast of the Presentation of Mary in the Temple, *Lumen Gentium* was approved. This document included a chapter on Mary.

On that same day at ceremonies in the Basilica of St. Mary Major in Rome, Pope Paul VI proclaimed the Blessed Mother to be the Mother of the Church. During the ceremonies, the pontiff recalled the consecration to the Blessed Virgin by Pope Pius XII on October 31, 1942, and personally renewed the consecration to her. Though it was a great thing to do, he did not have the collegial consecration requested by Our Lady of Fatima because the bishops were not all gathered together at the time.

Roughly two and a half years later, on the fiftieth anniversary of the first apparition at Fatima, May 13, 1967, Pope Paul VI delivered an apostolic exhortation to all of the bishops of the world, *Signum magnum* (The Great Sign). In it, the pontiff called for national diocesan and individual consecration to the Immaculate Heart of Mary.

The following October marked the twenty-fifth anniversary of Pope Pius XII's 1942 consecration of the Church and all of mankind to the Blessed Virgin Mary. At that time, Pope Paul VI exhorted all of the bishops to "renew personally their consecration to the Immaculate Heart of the Mother of the Church and to bring alive this most noble act of veneration through a life ever more consonant with the divine will and in a spirit of filial service and of devout imitation of their heavenly Queen."[8]

Pope Paul VI died eleven years later on August 6, 1978. Pope John Paul I was elected twenty days later but died a month after his election. Pope John Paul II would be elected as the next pontiff.

Pope John Paul II Makes the Consecration

Pope John Paul II would lead the Church into the new millennium. He had a great love for the Blessed Mother and said that reading St. Louis de Montfort's book *True Devotion to Mary* was a decisive point in his spiritual development. He took for his motto *Totus tuus* ("I am all yours").

Pope John Paul II possessed a charismatic personality and was a prolific writer, producing fourteen encyclicals, fourteen apostolic exhortations, eleven apostolic constitutions, forty-five apostolic letters, countless sermons, and other writings. He was involved with helping to revise canon law and the universal catechism called for by Vatican II. He was a well-traveled pope, bringing the love of Christ to many parts of the world. He had a special love for the youth and participated in World Youth days. This pontiff beatified and canonized more holy men and women than ever before.

Because of his personal background, Pope John Paul II understood Communism firsthand. Pope John Paul II recognized himself in the Third Secret as the bishop in white, and he would feel urged to carry out the consecration properly.

In his book *A Life with Karol,* Pope John Paul II's former secretary Cardinal Stanislaw Dziwisz describes the Blessed Mother's intervention to give back Pope John Paul II's life.

> In Sr. Lucia's vision, he recognized his own destiny. He became convinced that his life had been saved—no, given back to him anew—thanks to our Lady's intervention and protection.... It's true, of course, that "the bishop dressed in white" is killed in Sr. Lucia's vision, whereas John Paul II escaped an almost certain death. So? Couldn't that have been the real point of the vision? Couldn't it have been trying to tell us that the paths of history, of human existence, are not necessarily fixed in advance? And that there is a Providence, a "motherly hand," which can intervene and cause a shooter, who is certain of hitting his target, to miss?... "One hand shot, and another guided the bullet" was how the Holy Father put it.[9]

Pope John Paul II met with his would-be assassin Mehmet Ali Agca in person, whom he had already forgiven. Ali Agca wanted to know why his bullet did not kill the pope. Pope John Paul II believed wholeheartedly that the Blessed Mother guided the bullet. The bullet is now in the crown of the statue of Our Lady of Fatima in Portugal.

Pope John Paul II and the Consecration of Russia

To do the consecration that the Blessed Mother had requested, Pope John Paul II composed a beautiful prayer that he titled Act of Entrustment. He wanted it to be concelebrated in the Basilica of St. Mary Major on June 7, 1981, the Solemnity of Pentecost, which was the day chosen to commemorate the sixteen hundredth anniversary of the First Council of Constantinople and the 1,550th anniversary of the Council of Ephesus.

Pope John Paul II was unable to be present due to being in recovery from the bullet wounds, so he recorded the address to be broadcast.

Here is part of the Act of Entrustment, which references the world and Russia:

> *Mother of all individuals and peoples,* you know all their sufferings and hopes. In your motherly heart you feel all the struggles between good and evil, between light and darkness, that convulse the world: accept the plea which we make in the Holy Spirit directly to your heart, and *embrace with the love of the Mother and Handmaid of the Lord those who most await this embrace,* and *also those whose act of entrustment you too await in a particular way.* Take under your motherly protection the whole human family, which with affectionate love we entrust to you, O Mother. May there dawn for everyone the time of peace and freedom, the time of truth, of justice and of hope.[10]

The Holy Father desired to respond more fully to the requests of Our Lady of Fatima. His Act of Entrustment was repeated in an act of gratitude at Fatima on May 13, 1982. He wanted this consecration to be in union with the bishops of the Church, but the letters of invitation had not been sent to the world's bishops in time for them to participate. Though Pope John Paul II had beautiful and important things to say, including the urgency of the message of Fatima and that it seemed to be even more relevant then than in 1917, because the world's bishops were not participating, the consecration did not fulfill Our Lady of Fatima's request for the collegial union with all the bishops.

Almost two years later, in St. Peter's Square on March 25, 1984, the Solemnity of the Annunciation at the closing ceremony of the Holy Year of the Redemption, alongside numerous cardinals and bishops, and in union with all the bishops throughout the world, Pope John Paul II knelt before the statue of Our Lady of Fatima (which he requested be sent from the Fatima Chapel of Apparitions) and made the consecration requested by the Our Lady of Fatima. The bishops of the world had been convoked beforehand, and all people of the world were entrusted to the Immaculate Heart of Mary in his heartfelt words of 1981. Below are parts of the consecration prayer:

O Mother of all men and women, and of all peoples, you who know all their sufferings and their hopes, you who have a mother's awareness of all the struggles between good and evil, between light and darkness, which afflict the modern world, accept the cry which we, moved by the Holy Spirit, address directly to your Heart. *Embrace* with the *love* of the Mother and Handmaid of the Lord, this human world of ours, which we entrust and consecrate to you, for we are full of concern for the earthly and eternal destiny of individuals and peoples.

In a special way we entrust and consecrate to you those individuals and *nations* which particularly need to be thus entrusted and consecrated. "We have recourse to your protection, holy Mother of God!" *Despise not our petitions in our necessities....*

Behold, as we stand before you, Mother of Christ, before your Immaculate Heart, we desire, together with the whole Church, to unite ourselves with the consecration which, for love of us, your Son made of himself to the Father: "For their sake", he said, "I consecrate myself that they also may be consecrated in the truth" (John 17:19). We wish to unite ourselves with our Redeemer in this his consecration for the world and for the human race, which, in his divine Heart, has the power to obtain pardon and to secure reparation.

The power of this consecration lasts for all time and embraces all individuals, peoples and nations. It overcomes every evil that the spirit of darkness is able to awaken, and has in fact awakened in our times, in the heart of man and in his history.

How deeply we feel the need for the consecration of humanity and the world—our modern world—in union with Christ himself! For the redeeming work of Christ must be *shared in by the world through the Church*.... In entrusting to you, O Mother, the world, all individuals and peoples, we also *entrust* to you *this very consecration of the world*, placing it in your motherly Heart.

Immaculate Heart! Help us to conquer the menace of evil, which so easily takes root in the hearts of the people of today, and whose immeasurable effects already weigh down upon our modern world and seem to block the paths towards the future!...

Let there be revealed, once more, in the history of the world the infinite saving power of the Redemption: the power of *merciful Love*! May it put a stop to evil! May it transform consciences! May your Immaculate Heart reveal for all the *light of Hope!*"[11]

There has been controversy with regard to the way in which the consecration to Mary's Immaculate Heart was done. Some say it was not performed in accordance with the Blessed Mother's wishes. Still others have heard a variety of stories that are not true. It's important to have all of the facts and not listen to rumors.

Sister Lucia personally confirmed that this solemn and universal act of consecration was what Our Lady asked for. Specifically, she said, "Yes it has been done just as Our Lady asked, on 25 March 1984." In response to Sister Lucia's statement, the Congregation of the Doctrine of the Faith stated, "Hence any further discussion is without basis."[12]

A TIME TO REFLECT

Jacinta once reminded Lucia, "Tell everyone that God gives us His grace through His Mother's Immaculate Heart, which He wants to hold close to His own Sacred Heart. The people must ask for peace through Mary's Immaculate Heart, because that is the way God wants it, and that is what our Lady herself has told us!"

Where in the world do you think is most in need of the peace? Do you need peace in your own heart? What can you do to bring conflict and strife closer to the Immaculate Heart of Mary?

In My Own Life

What does the Immaculate Heart of Mary mean to you? Is there an image in your home? Did you consecrate your life to the Immaculate Heart of Mary?

You will find prayers of consecration in the Appendix and one below.

Prayer

Dear Lord God, please grant me your graces through the Immaculate Heart of Mary. Amen.

Here is a daily consecration prayer to the Immaculate Heart of Mary:

Queen of the Most Holy Rosary, I renew my consecration to you and to your Immaculate Heart. Please accept me, my dear Mother, and use me as you wish to accomplish your designs upon the world. I am all yours, my Mother, my Queen, and all that I have is yours.

Chapter Ten

THE IMPORTANCE OF THE FIVE FIRST
SATURDAY DEVOTION

I promise to help at the hour of death with the graces needed
for salvation, whoever, on the first Saturday of five consecutive
months shall confess and receive Holy Communion, recite five
decades of the rosary and keep me company for fifteen minutes
while meditating on the fifteen mysteries of the rosary.[1]

When the Blessed Mother appeared to the three visionaries, Lucia,
Francisco, and Jacinta—and later, just to Sister Lucia—she asked for
Five First Saturday devotion. Why did the Blessed Virgin Mary ask
her children (which is everyone in the world) to make the Five First
Saturday devotion?

What is the significance of this request? Why did she ask for five
and not nine, as in a novena, or why not thirteen as in the number
of Our Lady's sorrows? And why is the devotion done on Saturdays?

We will start with a very brief backdrop on the significance of
Saturdays with regard to the Blessed Mother. From the first centuries of the Church, Saturday was a specific day devoted to the Blessed
Virgin Mary. In the twelfth century, through St. Bernard, a new era
was born in the Church's devotion to the Mother of God. During his
lifetime this tireless saint established seventy Cistercian monasteries,
assisted at countless councils and synods, and preached a Crusade in
France. He was aided greatly by the Blessed Mother to accomplish
all of this work. He proclaimed, "When you follow Mary, there is
no straying from the way; when you pray to her, there is no cause to
despair; if she holds your hand, you will not fall; and if she protects
you, there is no need to fear."

It was St. Bernard who first suggested the theological foundation for the Church's consecration of Saturday to the Blessed Mother. He preached extensively on Mary, and in his seventh sermon on the Assumption, he said:

> In Mary alone did the faith of the Church remain steadfast during the three days that Jesus lay in the tomb. And although everyone else wavered, she who conceived Christ in faith, kept the faith that she had once for all received from God and never lost. Thus could she wait with assured hope for the glory of the Risen Lord.[2]

Later on, Thomas Aquinas reflected on the Third Commandment of the Decalogue and explained in detail why God ordered mankind to keep holy the Sabbath Day. St. Thomas taught: "Since the Resurrection took place on a Sunday, we keep holy this day instead of the Sabbath as did the Jews of old. However, we also sanctify Saturday in honor of the glorious Virgin Mary who remained unshaken in faith all day Saturday after the death of her Divine Son."[3]

St. Alphonsus Liguori (1696–1787), the founder of the Redemptorists, spoke about the Marian Saturday when he described various practices of piety in honor of the Blessed Virgin Mary in his classic work on *The Glories of Mary*. He writes:

> It is well known that Saturday has been set aside by the Church as Mary's Day because it was on the Sabbath after the death of her Son that she remained unshaken in her faith. For this reason, the clients of Mary are careful to honor her on that day by some particular devotion and especially by fasting....I affirm that those who practice this devotion can hardly be lost; not that I mean to say that if they die in mortal sin the Blessed Virgin will deliver them, but that those who practice it will, through Mary's help, find perseverance in God's grace easy and obtain from her a happy death. All the members of our little Congregation who are

able to do so practice this devotion. I say those who are able to do so; for if our health does not permit it, at least we should on Saturdays content ourselves with one dish at a meal, or observe an ordinary fast, or abstain from fruit, or something for which we have a relish. On Saturdays we should always practice some devotion in honor of Our Blessed Lady, receive Holy Communion, or hear Mass, visit an image of Mary, or something of that sort.[4]

Five First Saturdays

At Fatima, the Blessed Mother requested that the faithful pray a certain way on the First Saturdays of the month. She said it is necessary to pray in this way to hold off world problems as well as to save sinners. Even though the Queen of Heaven herself has requested this from us, sadly this devotion is considered the most forgotten part of the Fatima message.

Fr. Andrew Apostoli, CFR, wrote,

> As a mother, our Lady wants none of her children to be lost, but all to be saved. So, let us faithfully and generously carry out her wishes in this great devotion of the Five First Saturdays. Sister Lucia has assured us that prayer and penance are absolutely necessary for the peace of the world through the conversion of sinners. The Five First Saturdays devotion, with its unique combination of confession, Communion, and the Rosary, holds a special place in our Lady's plan.[5]

The Five First Saturdays are to make up for the five types of offenses committed against the Blessed Mother's Immaculate Heart. As was mentioned earlier, even Sister Lucia's confessor Fr. Jose Bernardo Goncalves, SJ, asked why we should make the First Saturday devotion. And, why is it for *five* Saturdays and not some other number? Sister Lucia wrote a letter to him on June 12, 1930, and described her encounter and conversation with the Lord in the chapel:

Remaining in the chapel with our Lord, part of the night of the 29th-30th of that month of May 1930, talking to our Lord about [some of those] questions, I suddenly felt possessed more intimately by the Divine Presence; and if I am not mistaken, the following was revealed to me: "Daughter, the motive is simple. There are five kinds of offenses and blasphemies spoken against the Immaculate Heart of Mary: blasphemies (1) against her Immaculate Conception; (2) against her perpetual virginity; (3) against her divine maternity, refusing at the same time to accept her as the Mother of mankind; (4) by those who try publicly to implant in the hearts of children an indifference, contempt, and even hate for this Immaculate Mother; and (5) for those who insult her directly in her sacred images.[6]

What if you've already made the Five First Saturdays? Why should you do it again? EWTN Chaplain Fr. Joseph Mary Wolfe explained in an EWTN newsletter article, "There is always a need for reparation. Although we can trust in the promises of Our Lady that we have satisfied her desires for ourselves personally, nonetheless, it will still be beneficial for us in making reparation for sins which continue against her Immaculate Heart and for obtaining world peace."[7]

Fr. Apostoli underscores our responsibility in this First Saturday devotion. "The Pope has done his part, but are we carrying out this devotion in sufficient numbers to bring about the conversion of sinners that Our Lady said would be needed for peace in the world?"[8]

A Time to Reflect

The Blessed Mother gave a huge promise to all mankind when she said, "I promise to help at the hour of death with the graces needed for salvation, whoever, on the first Saturday of five consecutive months shall confess and receive Holy Communion, recite five decades of the rosary and keep me company for fifteen minutes while meditating on the fifteen mysteries of the rosary."

The Five First Saturdays devotion isn't a magic formula, or a "get out of hell free" card for those who refuse to repent of serious sin! Rather, it is a holy path for those who want to practice their faith with greater fervor and purpose. To receive the graces of this devotion, we must be willing to open our hearts to the Holy Spirit, and be willing to give up those things that keep us from getting closer to God. What are some ways that you can prepare yourself to receive these graces not just at death, but for the rest of your life as well?

In My Own Life

Do you pray the rosary? Some people feel they don't have the time. Yet, it doesn't take as long to pray as we might be telling ourselves. I often break the rosary into decades because sometimes my schedule can be so demanding. But I don't want to get to the end of the day and lament that I haven't prayed it. Can I not take out about twenty minutes of my day to pray the rosary for Mother Mary?

Can you make the commitment to make the Five First Saturdays? Even if you have done so in the past, countless graces await you in the next Five First Saturdays. As well, countless souls can be saved by your small sacrifice. The Blessed Mother even guarantees to assist us at the hour of our deaths. Why are we not embracing this First Saturday Devotion? But, let's do it out of love for Our Lord, Our Lady, and to help save souls.

Prayer

Dear Lord Jesus, please help me to be an example to others and to be more generous with my time to pray. Blessed Mother Mary, please pray for me. St. Joseph, and all of the angels and saints, please pray for me. Amen.

Chapter Eleven

OUR LADY OF FATIMA'S IMPORTANCE TODAY

Throughout history there have been supernatural apparitions and signs which go to the heart of human events and which, to the surprise of believers and non-believers alike, play their part in the unfolding of history. These manifestations can never contradict the content of faith, and must therefore have their focus in the core of Christ's proclamation: the Father's love which leads men and women to conversion and bestows the grace required to abandon oneself to him with filial devotion. This too is the message of Fatima which, with its urgent call to conversion and penance, draws us to the heart of the Gospel. [1]

The message of Fatima is a call from the Mother of God for a renewed fidelity to penance and prayer and continual conversion of heart. She tells us to live the Gospel—to always "do whatever he tells you" (John 2:5). The Fatima message exemplifies Our Lord's desire that his Mother be better known, loved, and venerated through the devotion to her Immaculate Heart.

St. John Paul II said, "While the message of Our Lady of Fatima is a motherly one, it is also strong and decisive. It sounds severe. It sounds like John the Baptist speaking on the banks of the Jordan. It invites to repentance. It gives a warning. It calls to prayer. It recommends the rosary."[2]

At the time of the writing of this book, David Carollo, executive director of the World Apostolate of Fatima USA, has been to Fatima at least sixty times in the past thirty-five years. He explained to me, "When you travel to Fatima you not only come to understand the nature of the messages given by Our Lady ninety-nine years ago, but you see in the people who visit there a yearning for holiness." Carollo believes that this is what the Blessed Mother gave to the three children. Specifically, he said, "All of the predictions, warnings, and directions given there are meant to bring us to living in accord with the gospels. Personal holiness is what she is leading us to," he emphasized. "This is why the message of Fatima is the same today as it was in 1917."

What is the real and most essential message of the Fatima apparitions? If everything essential to our salvation was revealed to us in the time of the apostles, then why should we be given the messages of Fatima? Why does God periodically communicate through such mystics as St. Francis of Assisi, St. Catherine of Siena, and St. Teresa of Avila? Fr. Hardon says that it is not to reveal something unknown before but "to alert people to a revealed truth that had been ignored and that desperately needs to be met at certain periods of human history." In other words, we are people who need to be reminded—again and again.

Like Fr. Hardon, who claimed the greatest need today is "radical conversion from self-idolatry to faith in a loving God," the Blessed Mother at Fatima asserted that the sins of the world continue to grieve our Lord, and that we are called to pray for the souls of sinners. Lucia, Francisco, and Jacinta had to come to an understanding of the reality of hell in order for the message of the Blessed Mother to truly penetrate their hearts. We must do the same, for as Fr. Hardon says, "There is no real understanding of the essential message of Fatima unless we realize how deeply the modern world is steeped in sin."[3]

St. John Paul II expressed these facts during his three-day stay in Fatima in 1982. He said,

> Today, the successor of Peter…presents himself before the Mother of the Son of God at Fatima. In what way does he come?

He presents himself reading again with trepidation the motherly call to penance, to conversion, to the ardent appeal of the Heart of Mary that resounded at Fatima, sixty-five years ago. Yes, he reads it again with trepidation in his heart because he sees how many people and societies—how many Christians—have gone in the opposite direction to the one indicated in the message of Fatima. Sin has made itself firmly at home in the world, and denial of God has become widespread in the ideologies, ideas and plans of human beings.[4]

Does the end of the Cold War make Our Lady's message any less urgent or relevant for us today? Not at all. Russia's errors have certainly spread throughout the world in many ways. We live at a time when the idea of family is attacked, and there is a prevalent "culture of death" in which the sanctity of human life is assaulted. Abortion is rampant, as is euthanasia, assisted suicide, embryonic stem cell research, and more. Violence and hatred abounds. "It is important to recognize the connection between Communism and the culture of death," Fr. Apostoli wrote. He further explained, "Under atheistic Communism, Russia did not recognize the God-given dignity to human life. A person was important only to the degree that he was useful to the state." He continued, "Therefore, Russia became the first Christian nation in the world to permit abortion."[5]

The push for equality that characterized the system of Communism spread to Western Europe and the United States under different forms. For example, in the name of equality, the so-called "women's liberation movement" came into these countries, convincing women that in order to be equal to men in the workforce they needed "complete control over their ability to reproduce and that control included the power to kill their unborn children."[6]

As abortion became increasingly acceptable, the legalization of euthanasia began to eliminate the weak, elderly, or handicapped—those who were "not useful" or "valuable."

Yes, we need Mother Mary more than ever.

What Our Lady Requests

Through her Fatima messages, Our Lady requests a number of sincere actions from us that will benefit our own souls and the souls of others as well.

The Rosary: The Blessed Mother desires that we pray the rosary. "Pray the rosary every day in honor of Our Lady of the rosary to obtain peace in the world...for she alone can save it" (The Blessed Mother on July 13, 1917).

In all six of her apparitions at Fatima, the Blessed Mother emphasized the daily recitation of the rosary. Fr. Andrew Apostoli, CFR, believes that everyone can and should fulfill the Blessed Mother's requests by committing to praying the daily rosary. He also believes that Mary needs our prayers. Specifically, he wrote, "Our Lady told the children of the rosary's power to end wars, bring world peace and convert sinners. Everyone who wants to fulfill our Lady's requests at Fatima must make the resolution to pray the rosary every day. Remember, Mary wants our prayers; Mary needs our prayers for the triumph of her Immaculate Heart."[7]

The Immaculate Heart of Mary: Our Lady of Fatima asks us to become devoted to the Immaculate Heart of Mary. "Jesus wishes to establish devotion to my Immaculate Heart in the world. I promise salvation to those who embrace it" (The Blessed Mother on June 13, 1917).

Professor Americo Pablo Lopez-Ortiz, international president of the World Apostolate of Fatima, explained the Immaculate Heart of Mary as one of the greatest gifts from heaven and the spiritual presence of Mary with us through her Immaculate Heart. He said:

The Immaculate Heart of Mary represents the spiritual mother-hood of Mary over humanity. When she appeared to Sr. Lucia, Our Lady had the Heart in her hand and she offered her heart to Lucia. Lucia was representing all human beings when Our Lady said: "My heart will stay with you till the end." Our Lady was risen and assumed to heaven in body and soul, by her Son, Jesus Christ, but she left the Heart with us on earth: the heart is the spiritual presence of Mary. The spiritual action of the Mother is so much needed by her children. She wants to save her children. She has given us her heart. So her Immaculate Heart is with us on earth. We have two wonderful gifts from heaven. The most important one is the divine and real presence of Jesus Christ in the Most Blessed Sacrament: His body, blood, soul and Divinity, till the end of times. The second greatest gift is the spiritual motherhood of Mary given over humanity given to us by Jesus Christ on the First Good Friday, when Jesus said to his beloved disciple: "Behold your mother." From that moment on, John the beloved disciple of Christ, received Mother Mary in her Heart and in his own house.[8]

A Consecration to the Immaculate Heart of Mary: We are encouraged to consecrate our lives to the Immaculate Heart of Mary. Any formula can be used as long as it is sincere and confides oneself without reserve to the Blessed Mother. (See Appendix A for consecration prayers.)

Five First Saturdays: The Blessed Mother asks us to do our part and make the commitment to the Five First Saturdays devotion, which include: reception of Holy Communion and confession (within eight days before or after), to pray five decades of the rosary, and to spend fifteen minutes in meditation on the mysteries of the rosary to be offered up in reparation for sins and ingratitude against the Immaculate Heart of Our Lady.

Conversion: Transforming the world and establishing the Kingdom of God on earth begins with our own conversion of heart. We pray daily for graces to convert our hearts, to receive those graces and allow God to dwell in us in our interior life. Conversion of heart is an ongoing process. It is not just once in a lifetime. We need to pray every day for the conversion of our hearts so that we can become a brilliant light of God's love in a darkened world.

We are all called to conversion and holiness, not just the children at Fatima or someone else. St. Teresa of Calcutta often said, "Holiness is not the luxury of a few, but a simple duty for you and me."

With regard to the Fatima messages, in an interview on *EWTN Live*, Prof. Lopez-Ortiz said, "It is a great mistake to focus on the prophesies or what could happen at any moment in history...we would not be giving importance to what really matters. The same information available to the children is available to us too."

Host Fr. Mitch Pacwa, SJ, responded, "We need that kind of intimacy with God that they experienced."[9]

Reparation and Sacrifice: Our Lady of Fatima asks that we offer in reparation our own personal crosses and trials of life and to make sacrifices for the conversion of sinners, especially those sacrifices involved in keeping God's commandments, in patiently accepting God's will, and in fulfilling the duties of one's state in life. We are to offer them through the Immaculate Heart of Mary in reparation to God so offended by sin, and for the conversion of sinners. This instruction made a lasting impression on the young visionaries and should on us too.

"Sacrifice yourselves for sinners and say often whenever you make a sacrifice: 'O Jesus, it is for love of You, for the conversion of sinners, and in reparation for the offenses committed against the Immaculate Heart of Mary'" (The Blessed Mother on July 13, 1917). "Pray much and make sacrifices for sinners, for many souls go to hell because there is no one to make sacrifices for them" (The Blessed Mother on August 19, 1917).

How to Live Out the Heart of the Fatima Message

Conversion, prayer, and sacrifice are at the heart of the Fatima message. How do we live the message of Fatima? In his homily at Fatima, St. John Paul II quoted Scripture to drive home the message of Fatima's essential call to conversion and repentance:

> "Repent, and believe in the gospel" (Mark 1:15): these are the first words that the Messiah addressed to humanity. The message of Fatima is, in its basic nucleus, a call to *conversion and repentance*, as in the Gospel. This call was uttered at the beginning of the twentieth century, and it was thus addressed particularly to this present century. *The Lady of the message* seems to have read with special insight the "signs of the times," the signs of our time.[10]

One Hundred Years Later

Our Lady of Fatima appeared to three simple children in 1917 to profess an important and even urgent message to the world about the need to change our lives in accordance with the Gospels. The Blessed Mother also warned us of what would happen if the world did not stop offending God. She spoke of World War II, sufferings for the Church, and of Russia spreading its errors. Today the Church continues to be persecuted, the Holy Father has much to suffer, and errors were spread. Yet, we should be heartened knowing that Mary's Immaculate Heart will indeed triumph as she has promised.

What can we expect one hundred years later? In a personal interview, David Carollo of the World Apostolate of Fatima USA told me that he believes that though much disruption has happened, the tide can be turned. He said when Mary's Immaculate Heart will triumph, "we will see a great flood of grace in the world." Even though damage has been done, it is not too late to apply the Fatima messages to our lives. "Looking at our world in 2017," Carollo states, "we can see tremendous disruption everywhere. All of this is unnecessary, but we can turn the tide quickly if we commit ourselves to becoming reflections of the Blessed Mother and work to make reparation to God for our sinfulness." He continued, "God wants to show mercy to us, but we must sincerely ask for it. Perhaps a stronger awareness of this during the anniversary will bring about the conversion of hearts necessary to hasten the Triumph."

Fr. Andrew Apostoli, CFR, reflected on the one hundred years since the Blessed Mother appeared at Fatima in 1917 in a personal interview for this book. He said,

> To me it is amazing that one hundred years ago Our Lady warned of many things—Communism came, World Wars came during the one hundred years, the atomic bombs, concentration camps, Nazism, Fascism, Communism, Mao in China, Russia— all of these things happened in these hundred years that Satan had power. Now it seems to me only through Our Lady can this all be destroyed. And that is why Sister Lucia has said in her letter to Cardinal Caffara that Mary has already crushed the head of the serpent."

Fr. Apostoli was referring to a letter to Cardinal Carlo Caffara when he was archbishop of Bologna, Italy, in which Sister Lucia wrote, "The final battle between the Lord and the reign of Satan will be about marriage and the family." She added, "Don't be afraid, because anyone who works for the sanctity of marriage and the family will always be fought and opposed in every way, because this is the decisive issue, however, Our Lady has already crushed its head."[11]

Fr. Apostoli continued, "Back in 1884 in that vision that Pope Leo XIII had when he saw Christ, St. Michael, and the devil, and the devil was telling the Lord, 'I can destroy your Church, I just need more time and more power.' He was given one hundred years and unlimited power over his people."

Fr. Apostoli was speaking about the remarkable vision of Pope Leo XIII. It was October 13, 1884, exactly thirty-three years prior to the great Miracle of the Sun in Fatima, when Pope Leo XIII had a frightening vision which caused him to write the prayer of St. Michael. He had just finished celebrating Mass in his private chapel in the Vatican when the pontiff suddenly stopped at the foot of the altar. His face as white as a ghost, he waited and listened. He saw a vision of Satan approaching the throne of God and boasting that he could destroy the Church. Then, he immediately went to his office, sat down, and composed the prayer to St. Michael, with instructions that it be said after all low Masses everywhere.[12]

In 1886, Pope Leo XIII decreed that the St. Michael prayer be said at the end of low Mass (not high, or sung, Masses) throughout the universal Church, along with the *Salve Regina* (Hail, Holy Queen). This practice continued until about 1970, with the introduction of the new rite of the Mass.

Fr. Apostoli explained the significance of these one hundred years:

> One hundred years later is 1984. I believe that it was the conse-
> cration done by Pope John Paul II on March 25, 1984, which
> brought the blow that crushed the head of the serpent. Remember
> this, Communism, which had begun in Russia, was the primary
> tool of Satan in those one hundred years.
>
> Remember Our Lady in her July apparition? She talked about
> World War I ending; she talked about another war that would
> come if people didn't do what they were supposed to. She gave the
> sign of the unknown light. She then warned about an evil [that]
> will begin in Russia and spread throughout the world causing

wars and persecution of the Church, and everything else. That
evil was Communism. When the pope made the consecration—
I believe that's when Our Lady crushed the head of the serpent
in Russia—that was the source of Communism. And that's why
you don't hear about Communism anymore in Russia. Gorbachev
declared the Soviet Union ended in 1991 and gave freedom back
to those countries in Eastern Europe and so on.

In 1985, the year after the consecration, was the beginning
of increase of religion in Russia and churches opening—slowly,
because it was still under Communism domination. There was
a 375 percent increase in amount of churches, priests, and so
on. The monasteries increased from 120 in 1984 to over eight
hundred in 2011. If the devil had one hundred years, I think, and
this is my personal sense, that Our Lady took one hundred years
to bring about her triumph.

It required the consecration that was finally done. It was long
delayed, and that was a big problem. Secondly, she said, and this
is why we have to do our part with the rosary, the Five First
Saturdays devotion, the most important parts of Our Lady's
requests. She specifically asked for that as part of the conversion
of Russia, along with the consecration. She asked for two things
in the July apparition and people only talk about one—about the
consecration. They don't talk about the Five First Saturday devotion. That's our part.

Mary said, "When enough people do as I have said, my
triumph will come, and that will bring peace into the world." I
feel if you look at the world today we are in a tremendous position of an enormous explosion in this world between good and
evil. I think that is why Our Lady, the only one who can say this,
said when enough people do as I say, my triumph will come, and
that will bring peace into the world. If we don't do what she says, I

don't see where there is a great hope. But I do think something is going to happen in the year 2017 because it is the one hundredth anniversary.

There could be a chastisement first, could be an awful chastisement. St. Paul used to say we can't avoid the chastisement completely, but we can pray to mitigate it. I think if a chastisement comes and people start turning back to God, Mary can then bring her triumph.[13]

Our Duties to Live and Spread the Message of Fatima

One way that we can spread the message of Fatima is by living it. We are called to be an example of Christ's love and mercy. We can share the story and message of Fatima and pray for others to take it up and live it too.

Jesus told us that we must deny ourselves (turn away from our selfish ways), pick up our crosses, and follow him (Matthew 16:24), and St. Paul reminds us, "For our struggle is not against enemies of blood and flesh, but against the rulers, against the authorities, against the cosmic powers of this present darkness, against the spiritual forces of evil in the heavenly places" (Ephesians 6:12).

Though the reality of evil is scary, it is essential for us to acknowledge that we are engaged in a spiritual battle. It is because of this, Fr. Hardon argues, that the message of Fatima is an important one: "That is why the underlying strategy of Fatima is to urge the followers of Christ to use superhuman means to overcome the superhuman forces of evil that have been let loose on the world in our day."

How do we overcome evil forces? What is our weapon? It is supernatural grace, faith, prayer, repentance, and the rosary! We must heed the Blessed Mother's peace plan and do our part to spread her message. Our Lady of Fatima calls us to live lives of charity and to spread her message. Because of our duty to charity, we absolutely need to care about our fellow man. We need to care about others' souls and their eternal life.

In a personal interview for this book, EWTN's Colin Donovan, STL, said, "To the extent that it is the call of the Gospel, spreading it [the Fatima message] is possible to everyone in their own circumstances. Simply by standing up for the truth in the face of today's moral relativism one aligns oneself with the message of Fatima, and thus Our Lady and her Son."

But, is this enough? No, it is not. "We are asked to pray and do penance, specifically for those who, besides simply offending God by living sinful lives intentionally, oppose him, blaspheme him and the mysteries connected to him, especially regarding the Eucharist and the Mother of the Redeemer. This is doubly urgent because many of them are baptized Christians, often enough Catholics, who have sold their birthright for a pot of porridge," said Donovan.

The prayers taught to the three shepherd children are the very prayers we can pray in order to obtain conversion of sinners. Praying and suffering for others, especially those most in need, are true blessings and a great privilege. We can call to mind the two prayers that the Angel of Peace taught the children as well as both of the prayers that the Blessed Mother taught them. All four prayers speak of making reparation and atoning for sin, and helping those most in need.

Praying and offering to obtain conversion for sinners is, as Donovan points out, "to obtain the miracle of grace which is necessary for their conversion. This is our birthright, as members of the mystical body and the communion of the saints, to pray and suffer for our brothers and sisters in need, spiritual need, the greatest there is."

We are indeed blessed to have the message of Fatima. In fact, we have been given holy instructions, warnings, and heavenly promises.

"The Mother of the Lord was sent to restore us to her Son, and in warning us of the dangers, promised that 'in the end (her) Immaculate Heart would triumph.' Hope in that promise is hope in Christ,"[14] Donovan reminds us.

The story of Fatima involves holy simplicity, charity, and Truth. Three children from humble backgrounds possessed the faith and desire to believe. They desired to do good, to please God, and to help others. Like Mary herself, they answered "Yes!" to God through their encounters with the Angel of Peace and the Mother of God. Can we too give our wholehearted Yes?

Let us respond with great love to our Blessed Mother's requests that will indeed bring us closer to her Son Jesus as well as immensely help to save our neighbor's souls.

Totus Tuus!

A Time to Reflect

The message of Fatima is in reality a holy call from the Mother of God for a renewed fidelity to penance and prayer. The Blessed Mother tells us to live the Gospel—to always "do whatever he tells you" (John 2:5). The Fatima message is also Our Lord's message; he wants his Mother to be better known, loved, and venerated through the devotion to her Immaculate Heart.

We can never underestimate the miracles occurring in the hearts of the pilgrims visiting the Fatima Shrine. Pilgrims continue to travel from all parts of the world to experience Mary's loving touch at Fatima. As well, we can never fathom the unending miracles occurring in the hearts of all who pray sincerely and lovingly, striving to follow Our Lady of Fatima's peace plan. Mother Mary loves her children and touches all of our hearts.

How can we respond to Our Lady of Fatima's message today? We can offer our daily duties as well as sacrifices for the souls of sinners and pray the Fatima prayers as often as we can. We can pray the daily rosary, even if at times it needs to be prayed one decade at a time.

IN MY OWN LIFE

Our Lady of Fatima speaks to us about our responsibilities to prayer and to love. Are you loving your family members enough to care about their eternal salvation? This is truly our indispensable role in the family. What about your neighbors? Do you walk or drive by them but don't take time to get to know them? Do you pray for their salvation? Do you pray for your community? Do you make sacrifices and take time to pray for the needs of others?

Our Lady of Fatima is calling us to a renewed fidelity to penance and prayer. We need to step up to the plate. Now is the time. Our Lord and his Mother are counting on us.

PRAYER

Dear Lord Jesus, I want to give my life to you. I want to help to save souls with my sincere, loving prayers, sacrifices, penance, and actions. Dear Our Lady of Fatima, open my heart, my eyes, and ears to see the needs around me. Please pray for me and grant me the graces I need. Saint Joseph, all of the angels and saints, please pray for me. Amen!

As Divine Providence would have it, during the writing of this book many interesting things happened which I'll briefly tell you about. I am profoundly thankful for the outpouring of graces when writing this book. A few months before putting pen to paper to begin writing, I was extremely grateful to come across small relics of Francesco and Jacinta Marto. They had been given to me many years ago by a friend who visited Fatima. After finding them, I have always carried them with me in my purse. One time, just before giving a major talk at a popular Catholic conference, I took them out of my purse before-hand, kissed them, asking for the intercession of Blessed Francisco and Blessed Jacinta, and then showed them to my dear friend Fr. Andrew Apostoli, CFR, who was sitting right next to me at the evening event. He took them into his hands and also kissed them. I am deeply humbled and blessed that Fr. Apostoli, who is extremely knowledgeable about Fatima, has written the foreword for this book.

After being asked to write this book, Francisco's and Jacinta's relics were with me in my pocket continuously. I have deeply sensed their intercession and have asked for it throughout the writing. The vision-aries' relics have taken on a brand-new meaning for me.

On the eve of the anniversary of Our Lady of Fatima, I fractured my ribs and tore a muscle in a bizarre injury at the Hour of Great Mercy. It was a pain and suffering that I have offered up in the writing of this book. My thoughts went immediately to Jesus's abiding love, graces, and mercy as blood and water gushed forth from His side. As well, Sister Lucia was blessed with a vision of Jesus Crucified in which drops of Precious Blood from His face and a wound in His side fell into a chalice.

I don't think it is a coincidence that my husband and I were inspired to consecrate our home and family to the Sacred Heart of Jesus and to the Immaculate Heart of Mary during the writing of this book and specifically on the Feast of the Immaculate Heart of Mary. A beautiful image of the Sacred Heart of Jesus had always hung in our living room. One day, rummaging through a pile of pictures I had put aside for hanging "someday," I happened to come upon a stunning image of both Jesus and Mary, side-by-side—His Sacred Heart and her Immaculate one, and I absolutely knew that I needed to frame the image as soon as possible and then, along with my husband, consecrate our family and home. I strive to renew the consecration prayer with my husband on a regular basis.

As well, I don't think it is mere happenstance that on the weekend following our consecration to the hearts of Jesus and Mary, I came across a beautiful old framed picture of the Immaculate Heart of Mary at a flea market, of all places! It was the weekend of our wedding anniversary. I purchased the painting for just twelve dollars! It now hangs in my living room, where I often stand before it to say a prayer to Mother Mary, gazing and meditating upon her Immaculate Heart. Our Lady of Fatima proclaimed that in the end her Immaculate Heart will triumph! We can discover great hope in her words! I pray that you, dear reader, will receive many graces when reading this book and pondering and praying the Blessed Mother's Fatima message.

Finally, when this book was just about completed, something very exciting, and no doubt, providential happened. I met a woman named Maria Vida when I was making a short pilgrimage to the Divine Mercy Shrine in Stockbridge, Massachusetts. During our conversation at the shrine, I learned that Maria's older relatives were eyewitnesses of the Great Miracle of the Sun in Fatima. I was immensely intrigued and so happy to hear that news, believing in my heart that it was indeed providential that this amazing encounter should occur! Maria shared her thoughts with me. She said, "I feel very blessed that my Great Aunt and Uncle witnessed the Miracle of the Sun, for it helped us to be closer to Mary who points to Jesus and His Church." Maria said it is Mary's message and miracle that compels her to "pray the rosary every night." She believes, "we need to repent because Jesus was very much offended by our sins." She continued, "This miracle was very big. I don't understand why all Catholics are not paying attention to Mary's requests which will bring peace to the world," Maria put me right in touch with her cousin Mary Corda who could tell me exactly what had transpired in Fatima one hundred years ago.

Mary's grandparents were her mother's parents, Erminia and Antonio Caixeiro, and they were present in Fatima at the Cova da Iria on October 13, 1917. Ms. Cordo told me, "As early as I can remember my mother would tell us about the wonderful miracle that our Grandma and Grandpa saw in Portugal. We were given children's story of Fatima books and coloring books and we used to hear the story all the time." Ms. Cordo said her Grandfather died before she was born and added, "But my Grandmother used to confirm the story that my mother told us and would tell us how amazed she and her husband were at what they witnessed that day."

The Caixeiro couple lived in White Plains, New York, but for some time that year of 1917 they had been hearing about heavenly visits from their Portuguese relatives. Three shepherd children in Fatima were claiming to have seen the Blessed Mother appearing to them and said she predicted a great sign in October that year.

Ms. Cordo said, "They were planning a visit home [to Portugal] anyway, so they happened to be there in October and decided to make the trek to Fatima on the 13th to see what, if anything, was going to happen."

It was a long, arduous trip but Erminia and Antonia were determined to get to Fatima and see for themselves. It was about 134 miles from where they were visiting family in Reguengos de Fatal, Portugal. Ms. Cordo recounted, "They ended up walking quite a ways on foot in the pouring rain that was falling on the area that day. By the time they arrived at the Cova, they were drenched to the bone and covered in wet mud." According to Ms. Cordo, the persevering couple "made their way through the crowd, and found themselves about seventy-five feet or so from the three children, they couldn't get any closer than that due to the crowds."

Ms. Cordo continued to give me a blow-by-blow description of what her grandmother and mother had told her throughout her life about the Great Miracle.

> As they were standing there, the sun began to poke out from the clouds, then began to appear to swirl in the sky, then began to appear to hurl toward them. Many people screamed and dropped to their knees in fright and prayer, thinking it was truly the end of the world. The sun changed many colors—as each color came, the entire area was bathed in whatever color appeared. Then, the sun stopped spinning and appeared to go back up to its normal place, and things appeared to be normal once again, however, it was no longer raining, and when they looked down at themselves, they were no longer drenched to the bone, they were completely dry and their clothing was no longer muddy or dirty. It was clean!

Ms. Cordo's grandmother Erminia later told a reporter that she would never forget that day and recalled, "We were so scared."

Ms. Cordo has visited Fatima twice with her mother and plans to go back during the centennial year with her sisters. She believes wholeheartedly that her grandparents witnessing the Great Miracle of the Sun and her own "mother's example of unwavering and deep faith are what keeps the faithful tradition and devotion to Our Lady alive in me to this day." She believes it goes even deeper.

"And not just my devotion to Our Lady, but my whole Faith system as well. It is very hard to maintain connection with faith in today's age. There are so many distractions, and so many things to pull you away from your Faith roots. With this story and this strong family legacy, I can always come right back to it."

Ms. Cordo mentioned that in the time of her grandparents, the Cova da Iria in Fatima "was plain countryside...and now it is a grand square with buildings and a large cathedral." Ms. Cordo feels immensely connected to the story of Fatima and is happy that her "grandmother had told my mother approximately where she was standing on the day—she could estimate by lining up with the natural landmarks that still exist...my mother showed me the spot, and I hope to be able to remember it and show it to my two sisters when we go there next."

After witnessing the sun dancing in the sky at Fatima, Ms. Cordo's grandmother Erminia went on to speak about the Great Miracle of the Sun at many Fatima events, and whenever she returned to Fatima she was given the honor to carry the Portuguese flag in the Rosary procession.

An interview with this eyewitness appears in the original edition of John Haffert's book, *Meet the Witnesses*. I checked it out and found these compelling facts on page 80. Apparently this woman's story even affected the author of the Fatima book:

> An American witness who spoke freely to any visitor was Mrs. Erminia Caixeiro, of White Plains, NY. She became a daily Communicant after witnessing the miracle and returned to Fatima from America almost every year for the rest of her life. We met with her many times after this book was first published

in 1960. It was during one of those visits that I myself realized for the first time the greatness of the Fatima miracle.[1]

I find it to be rather amazing that this woman's eyewitness story unfolded before me through someone that I believe God placed in my path, and now it can be included in this book. Our Lord and Our Lady certainly provide.

Ms. Cordo concluded her testimony to me by saying, "Having this story as part of our family legacy has been one of my most treasured blessings in my life."

Fatima Prayers, Devotions, Shrines, Resources

Prayers
Prayers Associated with the Apparitions of Fatima
Angel of Peace Prayers

The Pardon Prayer

My God, I believe, I adore, I hope, and I love You! I beg pardon for those who do not believe, do not adore, do not hope, and do not love You. *(Pray three times.)*

The Angel's Prayer

Most Holy Trinity, Father, Son, and Holy Spirit, I adore You profoundly, and I offer You the most Precious Body, Blood, Soul, and Divinity of Jesus Christ, present in all the tabernacles of the world, in reparation for the outrages, sacrileges, and indifference with which He Himself is offended. And through the infinite merits of His Most Sacred Heart, and the Immaculate Heart of Mary, I beg of you the conversion of poor sinners. (*Pray three times.*)

Our Lady of Fatima Prayers

The Sacrifice Prayer

O Jesus, it is for love of You, and for the conversion of sinners and in reparation for the sins committed against the Immaculate Heart of Mary!

The Rosary Decade Prayer

O my Jesus, forgive us, save us from the fire of hell; lead all souls to Heaven, especially those who are most in need. (A version of the prayer commonly used in the US is: O my Jesus, forgive us our sins, save us from the fires of hell. Lead all souls to heaven, especially those in most need of Your mercy.)

THE EUCHARISTIC PRAYER

O most Holy Trinity, I adore You. My God, my God, I love You in the most Blessed Sacrament.

A Morning Offering

O Jesus,
  through the Immaculate Heart of Mary,
  I offer You my prayers, works,
  joys, and sufferings
  of this day for all the intentions
  of Your Sacred Heart,
  in union with the Holy Sacrifice of the Mass
  throughout the world,
  in reparation for my sins,
  for the intentions of all my relatives and friends,
  and in particular
  for the intentions of the Holy Father.
  Amen.

Prayer for the Canonization of Francisco and Jacinta Marto

Most Holy Trinity, Father, Son, and Holy Spirit, I adore You profoundly and I thank You for the Apparitions of the Most Holy Virgin in Fatima.

By the infinite merits of the Sacred Heart of Jesus and through the intercession of the Immaculate Heart of Mary I implore You—if it should be for Your greater glory and the good of our souls—to glorify in the sight of Your Holy Church Blessed Francisco and Jacinta, granting us through their intercession the grace which we implore.
  Amen.

(Then offer one Our Father, one Hail Mary, and one Glory Be.)[1]

The Prayers of the Rosary

"I am the Lady of the rosary," Our Lady of Fatima told the children.[2] The rosary is intimately linked with the message of Our Lady, who also told the children, "Continue to pray the rosary every day." Each time the Blessed Mother appeared to the young shepherd children in Fatima, she asked them to pray the daily rosary and offer their prayer for peace in the world.

"Pray the rosary every day in honor of Our Lady of the rosary to obtain peace in the world...for she alone can save it." (The Blessed Mother on July 13, 1917)

"God has placed peace in her hands, and it is from the Immaculate Heart that men must ask it." (Jacinta shortly before her death)

"When you pray the rosary, say after each mystery: 'O Jesus, forgive us our sins, save us from the fires of hell, lead all souls to Heaven, especially those who have most need of your mercy.' (The Blessed Mother first instructed them to include this prayer after each mystery when she appeared to them on June 13, 1917.)

Which mysteries should you pray each day?
There are four different sets of Mysteries commemorating the life of Christ which are meditated upon each day of the week, as follows:
- Sunday and Wednesday, outside of Lent and Advent: The Glorious Mysteries
- Monday and Saturday, and Sundays of Advent: The Joyful Mysteries
- Tuesday and Friday, and Sundays of Lent: The Sorrowful Mysteries
- Thursday: The Mysteries of Light

THE JOYFUL MYSTERIES:
First Mystery: The Annunciation of the Angel to Our Lady (Luke 1:26–38)
Second Mystery: The Visitation of Our Lady to Saint Elizabeth (Luke 1:39–56)
Third Mystery: The Birth of Jesus in Bethlehem (Luke 2:1–20)

Fourth Mystery: The Presentation of the Child Jesus in the Temple (Luke 2:22–38)

Fifth Mystery: The Finding of the Child Jesus in the Temple with the Doctors (Luke 2:41–50)

THE MYSTERIES OF LIGHT:[3]

First Mystery: The Baptism of Jesus in the Jordan (Matthew 3:13–17)

Second Mystery: The Revelation of Jesus during the Wedding in Cana (John 2:1–11)

Third Mystery: The Proclamation of God's Kingdom and the Call to Conversion (Mark 1:14–15)

Fourth Mystery: The Transfiguration of the Lord (Luke 9:28–36)

Fifth Mystery: The Institution of Eucharist (Luke 22:14–20)

THE SORROWFUL MYSTERIES:

First Mystery: The Agony of Jesus in the Garden (Matthew 26:36–46)

Second Mystery: The Scourging of Jesus (Matthew 27:24–26)

Third Mystery: The Crowning with Thorns (Matthew 27:27–31)

Fourth Mystery: Jesus's Way to Calvary and the Meeting with His Mother (Luke 23:26–32)

Fifth Mystery: The Crucifixion and Death of Jesus (John 19:17–30)

THE GLORIOUS MYSTERIES:

First Mystery: The Resurrection of Jesus (Matthew 28:1–10)

Second Mystery: The Ascension of Jesus to Heaven (Acts 1:6–11)

Third Mystery: The Descent of the Holy Spirit on Our Lady and the Apostles (Acts 1:12–14; 2:1–4)

Fourth Mystery: The Assumption of Our Lady (Luke 1:48–49)

Fifth Mystery: The Coronation of Our Lady as Queen of Heaven and Earth (Revelation 12:1–17)

How do I pray the Rosary?

Begin by holding the rosary beads in your hands and gently kissing the cross. Then make the Sign of the Cross and say, "In the name of the Father, and of the Son, and of the Holy Spirit. Amen."

Then, holding the crucifix, say the Apostles' Creed.

> I believe in God, the Father Almighty, Creator of heaven and earth; and in Jesus Christ, His only Son, Our Lord, who was conceived by the Holy Spirit, born of the Virgin Mary, suffered under Pontius Pilate, was crucified, died, and was buried. He descended into Hell; on the third day He rose again from the dead; He ascended into Heaven, and is seated at the right hand of God, the Father almighty; from there He shall come to judge the living and the dead. I believe in the Holy Spirit, the holy catholic Church, the communion of saints, the forgiveness of sins, the resurrection of the body and life everlasting. Amen.

1. First large bead. Pray the Our Father:

> Our Father, Who art in heaven, Hallowed be Thy Name; Thy Kingdom come; Thy Will be done, on earth as it is in Heaven. Give us this day our daily bread; and forgive us our trespasses as we forgive those who trespass against us; And lead us not into temptation, but deliver us from evil. Amen.

2. On next three (small) beads, pray three Hail Marys and ask for an increase in the virtues of faith, hope, and charity. Conclude with a Glory Be.

> Hail Mary, full of grace, the Lord is with thee; blessed art thou among women, and blessed is the fruit of thy womb, Jesus. Holy Mary, Mother of God, pray for us sinners, now and at the hour of death. Amen.

* * *

> Glory be to the Father, and to the Son, and to the Holy Spirit. As

it was in the beginning, is now, and ever shall be, world without end. Amen.

3. For each of the five decades, on the large bead (or medallion) announce the Mystery, with a brief reading from Scripture, if desired. Then pray the Our Father.

4. On each of the ten smaller beads of each decade, pray a Hail Mary while meditating on the Mystery for that decade. Then pray a Glory Be.

5. After finishing each decade, you may add the Fatima Prayer, which was requested by the Blessed Virgin Mary at Fatima:

O my Jesus, forgive us our sins, save us from the fires of hell; lead all souls to Heaven, especially those who have most need of your mercy.

6. After completing the five decades, pray the Hail, Holy Queen:

Hail, holy Queen, mother of mercy, our life, our sweetness, and our hope. To thee do we cry, poor banished children of Eve. To thee do we send up our sighs, mourning and weeping in this valley of tears. Turn then, most gracious advocate, thine eyes of mercy toward us, and after this our exile show us the blessed fruit of thy womb, Jesus. O clement, O loving, O sweet Virgin Mary.
(Leader) Pray for us, O Holy Mother of God.
(Response) That we may be made worthy of the promises of Christ.
(Leader) Let us pray:
(Response) O God, whose Only Begotten Son, by his life, death, and resurrection, has purchased for us the rewards of eternal life, grant, we beseech thee, that while meditating on these mysteries of the most holy rosary of the Blessed Virgin Mary, we may imitate what they contain and obtain what they promise, through the same Christ our Lord. Amen.

You can say the following if desired: Most Sacred Heart of Jesus, have mercy on us. Immaculate Heart of Mary, pray for us.

7. Conclude the rosary with the Sign of the Cross.

When the rosary is said in a group or individually prayed before the Blessed Sacrament, you may gain a plenary indulgence under the usual conditions, which includes prayer for the intentions of the Holy Father (on the first three small beads in the opening prayers of the rosary). However, the primary spiritual benefit of the rosary is perhaps best expressed in this teaching from the United States Conference of Catholic Bishops: "The repetition in the rosary is meant to lead one into restful and contemplative prayer related to each Mystery. The gentle repetition of the words helps us to enter into the silence of our hearts, where Christ's spirit dwells."[4]

Devotions and Practices Associated with Fatima
Consecration to the Immaculate Heart of Mary Prayer
Any formula may be used to consecrate oneself to Mary, the Mother of God, as long as it is sincere and involves a total oblation of oneself. One of the following consecrations could be renewed each first Saturday for five consecutive months, with the shorter formula renewed daily.

First Saturday Prayer
O Virgin Mary, most powerful Mother of Mercy, Queen of Heaven and earth, in accordance with your wish made known at Fatima, I consecrate myself today to your Immaculate Heart. To you I entrust all that I have, all that I am. Reign over me, dearest Mother, that I may be yours in prosperity, in adversity, in joy and in sorrow, in health and in sickness, in life and in death.

Most compassionate Heart of Mary, Queen of Virgins, watch over my mind and heart and preserve me from the deluge of impurity which you lamented so sorrowfully at Fatima. I want to be pure like you. I want to atone for the many crimes committed against Jesus and you. I want to call down upon this country and the whole world the peace of God in justice and charity.

Mindful of this consecration, I now promise to strive to imitate you by the practice of the Christian virtues without regard for human respect. I resolve to receive Holy Communion on the first Saturday of every month when possible, and to offer daily five decades of the rosary, with all my sacrifices in the spirit of penance and reparation. Amen.

Daily Prayer of Consecration

I, ..., a faithless sinner, renew and ratify today in thy Heart, O Immaculate Mother, the vows of my Baptism; I renounce forever Satan, his pomps and works; and I give myself entirely to Jesus Christ, the Incarnate Wisdom, to carry my cross after Him all the days of my life, and to be more faithful to Him than I have ever been before.

Queen of the Most Holy Rosary, in the presence of all the heavenly court, I choose thee this day for my Mother and Mistress. I deliver and consecrate to thee, and to thy Immaculate Heart, as thy child and slave of love, my body and soul, my goods, both interior and exterior, and even the value of all my good actions, past, present and future; leaving to thee the entire and full right of disposing of me, and all that belongs to me, without exception, according to thy good pleasure, for the greater glory of God, in time and in eternity. Amen.

Shorter Daily Renewal of Consecration to the Immaculate Heart of Mary

Queen of the Most Holy Rosary, I renew my consecration to you and to your Immaculate Heart. Please accept me, my dear Mother, and use me as you wish to accomplish your designs upon

the world. I am all yours, my Mother, my Queen, and all that I
have is yours.

Pilgrim Statue Devotions

Every year on the anniversary of Our Lady of Fatima, May 13, as
well as on the thirteenth of the months thereafter through October,
the "miraculous Statue" of Our Lady of Fatima ("Pilgrim Statue"),
which stands atop of a pillar that marks the exact spot of the apparitions, is removed by a designated person with gloved hands. It is
then processed on a carrier on the shoulders of eight men, four on
each side, through the Cova da Iria and to the altar where the holy
Mass will be offered. Hundreds of thousands of pilgrims come from
all over the globe to show their love to the Virgin Mary, who always
leads us to her Son Jesus.

Two twin statues were sculpted in 1947 by Jose Thedim following
precise instructions from Sister Lucia. The first Pilgrim Virgin Statue
left Fatima in May 1947 to travel through Europe. The first statue is
now retired and on display at the Basilica of Our Lady of Fatima in
Portugal.

The second twin statue was blessed by the Bishop of Leiria-Fatima
on October 13, 1947, in the presence of two hundred thousand
pilgrims. The Bishop prayed that the Blessed Virgin would accom-
pany the statue wherever it traveled.

The purpose of the Pilgrim Virgin Statue tour is to bring Fatima
graces all over the world to benefit people who cannot visit Fatima.
The statue has visited more than one hundred countries, including
Russia and China.

I asked Patrick L. Sabat, the present principal statue custodian,
about miracles associated with the statue. He told me, "It is God
that performs the miracles through the intercession of Our Lady....
In many cases, when the people refer to the 'miraculous' statue it is
because it shed tears in the past; some were documented just like one
instance in Louisiana."

Sabat shared his experiences with the Pilgrim statue. He said, "My whole life has been a pilgrimage with the Blessed Mother, literally, as I take the statue around the world. Figuratively, she takes me on a pilgrimage with her Son." Sabat continuously renews his consecration to the Blessed Mother.

Sabat is deeply moved by the testimonies from the countless people he meets around the world who receive graces of conversion, as well as miracles of physical healing. Among the many testimonies, Sabat told me about a man in Detroit who helped him carry the statue. The man had been crippled with shoulder pain for thirty years but did not tell Sabat when he was asked to help with the statue. Nine years later, he saw Sabat again and told him how he had been miraculously healed of the condition and has not taken his pain medication since.

Another miracle that Sabat shared with me involved a mother of five with two estranged children. During the visit of the Pilgrim Statue, both children called their mother out of the blue. The second one called at two in the morning. The mother reluctantly answered the phone. Her daughter said, "Mom, had you not answered the phone, I would have ended my life."

The Pilgrim Fatima Statue travels around the world, making visits to dioceses, parishes, and even private homes. You can learn more details and about the schedule online.[5]

Why do those in the crowd wave white handkerchiefs?

If you have ever seen the procession, you have probably seen the affectionate gesture of thousands of pilgrims waving white handkerchiefs. I inquired about this practice. EWTN's Colin Donovan, STL, explained it to me:

> As I understand it, the waving of white handkerchiefs developed as a spontaneous gesture of the people at the end of the apparitions. It would seem to have meant Mary's departure. However,

for the Portuguese today it is reserved as a sign of affection for Our Lady on the occasion of their own departure for their homes. It is seen predominantly, therefore, at the end of the Mass of the thirteenth of May to October, when the statue is carried from the altar to the Capelinha, the 'little chapel' of the apparitions. The beautiful hymn *Adeus*, which is sung at this time, reflects this as well.

Fr. Michael Joseph Russo, pastor of Our Lady of Fatima parish in Lafayette, Louisiana, decided to bring the waving of the white handkerchief tradition into his own parish. He explained:

> We started the thirteenth of the month Fatima Novena Masses, from May through October, and introduced the Fatima Farewell Procession. For years now, parishioners wave their white handkerchiefs at the end of Mass during the final procession with Our Lady's statue while singing the Fatima Farewell Hymn—just as they do at the Fatima Shrine. There's always a row of teary-eyed men and women as Our Lady makes her way down the aisle.

In his book *The Intimate Life of Sister Lucia*, Fr. Robert J. Fox wrote about the waving of the handkerchiefs. He said:

> The Farewell "Adeus" Procession at the greater processions after Mass and Benediction/Blessing of the Sick is a ceremony which is moving for most people....These people are well aware, as the "Adeus" is sung, that the miraculous Statue moving through the crowds, returning to her place atop the pillar site of the Apparitions, is not Our Lady herself. But they sense some special moral presence of Mary at this time in this touching ceremony. They raise their voices strongly in "O Fatima, Farewell." Not a few tears are shed and the waving of the handkerchiefs appear to be a sea of white doves flying over the crowds. Not infrequently actual doves join the festivities and are seen at this time flying over the

Cova and occasionally even around the statue, even landing at the feet of Our Lady.[6]

What is the "Miracle of the Doves"?

A fascinating phenomenon has occurred in conjunction with the processing Pilgrim Statue at Fatima. On numerous occasions, white doves have alighted on the statue as well as on the altar for Mass. When asked about the mysterious "Miracle of the Doves," EWTN's Colin Donovan, STL, who has seen the doves himself, tells the story this way:

> The first recorded instance of the Miracle of the Doves seems to have been December 1, 1946. That day the statue of Our Lady was started in procession from Fatima to Lisbon, for the celebration of the third centenary of Portugal's consecration in 1646 to the Immaculate Heart by King João (John) IV. As the procession began, four doves were released to commemorate the occasion. One of them flew away, but three flew to the foot of the statue, where they remained, without eating, drinking, or moving from their places for the entirety of the seventy-mile trip to Lisbon.

> Along the way, as it passed through the many villages, crowds lined the roads, the bearers would be periodically changed, but the doves never left, even when fireworks were part of the celebratory atmosphere.

> On the evening of December 7 in Lisbon, a candlelight procession and Mass was held at the Cathedral with the Cardinal Patriarch as celebrant. At the Mass the doves could be seen moving. Then, at the ringing of the bell preceding the consecration, one of the doves flew to the right side of the altar, while another flew to the left side. The middle of the three remained at the base of the statue. When the celebrant began to elevate the Host, they both alighted on the altar and folded their wings, as if adoring. They remained there unmoving as the Mass continued.

Finally, at communion time, the third dove, which had remained at the foot of Our Lady's statue, flew to the crown of the statue and, as the "Behold the Lamb of God" was pronounced, opened its wings and held them open.

While the Miracle of the Doves has not repeated itself in exactly the same way, as far as I know, the phenomenon of doves alighting on the statue and being immovable from it has been observed on innumerable occasions in Fatima, as well as in connection with the Pilgrim Virgin Statue in other parts of the world. I have observed it myself on several occasions in Fatima, beginning with May 13, 1982, when Pope John Paul II came to give thanks for his surviving an assassin's bullet, and to consecrate the world to the Immaculate Heart.

Consecration of the World and Ourselves to Jesus through the Immaculate Heart of Mary

As we discussed, Our Lady of Fatima called for a consecration of the world to her Immaculate Heart. We can also consecrate ourselves individually to Jesus through Mary. You can see suggested consecration prayers in the prayer section a little earlier in this Appendix.

St. John Paul II explained what the consecration means in his homily on the sixty-fifth anniversary of Fatima. He brings us back to the redemptive cross and Jesus's gift of his Mother Mary to us:

On the Cross Christ said: "Woman, behold, your son!" With these words he opened in a new way his Mother's heart. A little later, the Roman soldier's spear pierced the side of the Crucified One. That pierced heart became a sign of the redemption achieved through the death of the Lamb of God.

The Immaculate Heart of Mary, opened with the words "Woman, behold, your son!", is spiritually united with the heart of her Son opened by the soldier's spear. Mary's Heart was opened by the same love for man and for the world with which Christ loved man and the world, offering himself for them on the Cross, until the soldier's spear struck that blow.

Consecrating the world to the Immaculate Heart of Mary means drawing near, through the Mother's intercession, to the very Fountain of life that sprang from Golgotha. This Fountain pours forth unceasingly redemption and grace. In it reparation is made continually for the sins of the world. It is a ceaseless source of new life and holiness.

Consecrating the world to the Immaculate Heart of the Mother means returning beneath the Cross of the Son. It means consecrating this world to the pierced Heart of the Savior, bringing it back "to the very source of its Redemption." Redemption is always greater than man's sin and the "sin of the world." The power of the Redemption is infinitely superior to the whole range of evil in man and the world.

The Heart of the Mother is aware of this, more than any other heart in the whole universe, visible and invisible. And so she calls us. She not only calls us to be converted: she calls us to accept her motherly help to return to the source of Redemption.

Consecrating ourselves to Mary means accepting her help to offer ourselves and the whole of mankind to *Him who is Holy*, infinitely Holy; it means accepting her help by having recourse to her motherly Heart, which beneath the Cross was opened to love for every human being, for the whole world in order to offer the world, the individual human being, mankind as a whole, and all the nations to Him who is infinitely Holy. God's holiness showed itself in the redemption of man, of the world, of the whole of mankind, and of the nations: a redemption brought about through the Sacrifice of the Cross. "For their sake I *consecrate myself*," Jesus had said (John 17:19).

By the power of the redemption the world and man *have been consecrated.* They have been consecrated to Him who is infinitely Holy. They have been offered and entrusted to Love itself, merciful Love.

The Mother of Christ calls us, invites us to join with the Church of the living God in the consecration of the world, in this act of confiding by which the world, mankind as a whole, the nations, and each individual person are presented to the Eternal Father with the power of the Redemption won by Christ. They are offered in the Heart of the Redeemer which was pierced on the Cross.[7]

St. John Paul II's words give us much to ponder. Indeed, we need to change our lives and open our hearts to conversion. St. John Paul II reminds us, "And so she calls us. She not only calls us to be converted: she calls us to accept her motherly help to return to the source of Redemption."

Let us pray to draw closer to Mary's Immaculate Heart. We need Mary now more than ever.

SHRINES AND RESOURCES

The Shrine in Fatima, Portugal

http://www.santuario-fatima.pt/en

The Shrine of Our Lady of the Rosary of Fatima is the answer to the call of Our Lady of the Rosary, already alluded to, on the thirteenth of August 1917 and expressly asked in the apparition of the thirteenth of October of that year to Lucia de Jesus, Francisco Marto, and Jacinta Marto: "*I want to tell you that a chapel is to be built here in my honor. I am the Lady of the Rosary*" (First Memoir of Sister Lucia).

The little chapel was constructed in 1919 at the location of the apparitions of 1917 at the Cova da Iria. Since then, the place of the Shrine has been built up, in response to a significant influx of pilgrims.

The Shrine of Fatima is, by an expressed will of the Apostolic See, a national shrine.

The World Apostolate of Fatima, USA

http://wafusa.org

David Carollo, executive director of The World Apostolate of Fatima, described the association in this way: "It is a Public Association of the Faithful in the Church. Founded as The Blue Army of Our Lady of Fatima in 1947, we are now an international association with a presence in one hundred countries. We are the official voice of The Church on Fatima. We work with our priests and bishops promoting this message for hope for the world."

The Message of Fatima is a document from the Congregation of the Doctrine of the Faith that describes what the Church teaches about the messages and secrets of Fatima, and their authentic meaning. It includes copies of actual letters from Sister Lucia, Pope John Paul II, and more. It is available online at the Vatican website.[8]

Fatima for Today: The Urgent Marian Message of Hope by Fr. Andrew Apostoli, CFR, is an invaluable resource that provides an in-depth historical and theological treatment of the apparitions of Fatima and their importance for today.

OUR LADY'S MESSAGE ON THE ROSARY

The practice of using strings of beads to count prayers and to aid in meditation originated in the earliest days of the Church, with roots in pre-Christian times. The origin of the rosary dates back hundreds of years. There is evidence that strings of beads were used to count Our Fathers and Hail Marys even in the Middle Ages.

Tradition holds that the Blessed Mother appeared to St. Dominic (d. 1221) and impressed upon him that the rosary is the only prayer to fight heresy in his missionary work. Many of the saints and popes were devoted to praying the rosary and encouraged its devotion.

Sister Lucia expressed, "The Most Holy Virgin in these last times in which we live has given a new efficacy to the recitation of the rosary to such an extent that there is no problem, no matter how difficult it is, whether temporal or above all spiritual, in the personal life of each one of us, of our families...that cannot be solved by the rosary. There is no problem, I tell you, no matter how difficult it is, that we cannot resolve by the prayer of the Holy Rosary."

Pope Pius IX said, "Give me an army saying the rosary and I will conquer the world." Pope St. Pius X said, "The rosary is the most beautiful and the most rich in graces of all prayers; it is the prayer that touches most the Heart of the Mother of God...and if you wish peace to reign in your homes, recite the family rosary." St. Pio of Pietrelcina (Padre Pio) said, "The rosary is *the* weapon."

St. Louis de Montfort passionately extolled the power of the prayer of the rosary. He said, "If you say the rosary faithfully unto death, I do assure you that, in spite of the gravity of your sins, 'you will receive a never-fading crown of glory' (1 Peter 5:4)." He even went so far as to say, "Even if you are on the brink of damnation, even if you have one foot in hell, even if you have sold your soul to the devil as sorcerers do who practice black magic, and even if you are a heretic as obstinate as a devil, sooner or later you will be converted and will amend your life and will save your soul, if—and mark well what I say—if you say the Holy rosary devoutly every day until death for the purpose of knowing the truth and obtaining contrition and pardon for your sins."

Fr. John A. Hardon, SJ, made clear about the rosary, "It is no mere repetition of Hail Marys or even just a pious practice of devout Catholics. It is—or should be—a daily reflection on the revealed truths which undergird the whole edifice of the Catholic Church. Without these truths, nothing in Catholicism makes sense; with these truths, everything in our religion holds together."[1]

John Paul II and the Rosary

St. John Paul II wrote a beautiful Apostolic Letter about the rosary called *Rosarium Virginis Mariae* on October 16, 2002, the beginning of the twenty-fifth year of his pontificate. Reading this document, we can sense his great love for the Virgin Mary:

The rosary of the Virgin Mary, which gradually took form in the second millennium under the guidance of the Spirit of God, is a prayer loved by countless Saints and encouraged by the Magisterium. Simple yet profound, it still remains, at the dawn of this third millennium, a prayer of great significance destined to bring forth a harvest of holiness. It blends easily into the spiritual journey of the Christian life, which, after two thousand years, has lost none of the freshness of its beginnings and feels drawn by the Spirit of God to "set out into the deep" (duc in altum!) in order once more to proclaim, and even cry out, before the world that Jesus Christ is Lord and Savior, "the way, and the truth and the life" (John 14:6), "the goal of human history and the point on which the desires of history and civilization turn" (RVM 1).

He ended *Rosarium Virginis Mariae* with a loving call to action meant for each and every one of us:

I look to all of you, brothers and sisters of every state of life, to you, Christian families, to you, the sick and elderly, and to you, young people: *confidently take up the rosary once again.* Rediscover the rosary in the light of Scripture, in harmony with the Liturgy, and in the context of your daily lives.

May this appeal of mine not go unheard! At the start of the twenty-fifth year of my Pontificate, I entrust this Apostolic Letter to the loving hands of the Virgin Mary, prostrating myself in spirit before her image in the splendid Shrine built for her by Blessed Bartolo Longo, the apostle of the rosary. I willingly make my own the touching words with which he concluded his well-known Supplication to the Queen of the Holy rosary: "O Blessed Rosary of Mary, sweet chain which unites us to God, bond of love which unites us to the angels, tower of salvation against the assaults of Hell, safe port in our universal shipwreck, we will never abandon you. You will be our comfort in the hour of death: yours our final kiss as life ebbs away. And the last word from our lips will be your sweet name, O Queen of the Rosary of Pompeii, O dearest Mother, O Refuge of Sinners, O Sovereign Consoler of the Afflicted. May you be everywhere blessed, today and always, on earth and in heaven (RVM 43).

I recommend reading the apostolic letter in its entirety. It is available online on the Vatican website. I humbly and wholeheartedly echo Blessed Bartolo Longo's and St. John Paul II's touching sentiments above. May we all call upon our sweet and powerful Mother Mary today and always. *Totus tuus!*

NOTES

PREFACE

1. Archbishop Tarcisio Bertone, SDB, "The Message of Fatima," 4, http://www.vatican.va/roman_curia/congregations/cfaith/documents/rc_con_cfaith_doc_20000626_message-fatima_en.html.

CHAPTER ONE

1. John Paul II, "Homily at Fatima, Portugal" on May 13, 1982, *L'Osservatore Romano,* Weekly Edition in English, May 17, 1982.
2. John Paul II, "Homily at Fatima."
3. Andrew Apostoli, CFR, "The Woman He Loved: Fulton Sheen and the Blessed Mother," Archbishop Fulton Sheen Centre, http://archbishopful-tonsheencentre.com/Mother_Mary.htm.
4. John A. Hardon, SJ, "The Doctrinal Message of Fatima," John A. Hardon, SJ Archives, The Real Presence Association, http://www.therealpresence.org/archives/Church_Dogma/Church_Dogma_041.htm
5. John Paul II, "Mary's Message of Love," 5, EWTN, http://www.ewtn.com/library/PAPALDOC/JP820513.HTM.
6. John Paul II, "Mary's Message of Love," 5.
7. John Paul II, "Homily at Fatima."
8. David Carollo (executive director, World Apostolate of Fatima U.S.A.), in interview with the author, August 12–16, 2016.
9. Hardon, "The Doctrinal Message of Fatima."
10. Benjamin Mann, "On Fatima anniversary, Fr. Apostoli sees atheism overtaking the West," *EWTN News,* October 13, 2011.
11. Teresa of Calcutta to Calcutta's Archbishop Perier, SJ, December 3, 1947.
12. Filipe d'Avillez, "Mother Teresa had a very good sense of humor," *Actualidade Religiosa,* May 10, 2016.
13. David Scott, "Mother Teresa's Long Dark Night," *The Love That Made Mother Teresa* (Manchester, NH: Sophia Institute, 2013), 107–113.
14. Scott, 107–113.
15. Renzo Allegri, "Mother Teresa's Secret Effort to Consecrate Russia," Patheos, July 15, 2016, http://www.patheos.com/blogs/mysticpost/2016/07/16/mother-teresas-secret-effort-to-consecrate-russia/.
16. Allegri, "Mother Teresa's Secret Effort to Consecrate Russia."
17. John Paul II, "Mary's Message of Love," 2.

CHAPTER TWO

1. Sister Lucia of Jesus and the Immaculate Heart, *"Calls" from the Message of Fatima,* trans. Sisters of Mosteiro de Santa Maria and Convento de

N.S. do Bom Sucesso, Lisbon (N.p.: Coimbra Carmel and Fatima Shrine, 2001), 44.

2. Lucia dos Santos, *Fatima, in Lucia's Own Words: Sister Lucia's Memoirs,* ed. Louis Kondor, S.V.D., trans. Dominican Nuns of Perpetual Rosary (N.p.: Fatima Postulation Center, 1976), 76.

3. Dos Santos, 62.

4. Dos Santos, 62.

5. Dos Santos, 170 –171.

6. Andrew Apostoli, CFR, *Fatima For Today: The Urgent Marian Message of Hope* (San Francisco: Ignatius, 2010), 25.

7. Dos Santos, 152.

8. Dos Santos, 152.

9. Dos Santos, 152.

10. Dos Santos, 152.

11. Dos Santos, 152, 154.

12. Joseph Pronechen, "Fatima for Today : Pope John Paul II Was Serious About Mary's Requests," National Catholic Register, April 29, 2011.

13. John Baptist Vianney, "Sermon on Communion," *Sermons of the Cure of Ars* (Charlotte, NC: Tan, 1995).

14. Donna-Marie Cooper O'Boyle, *Bringing Lent Home with Pope Francis: Prayers, Reflections, and Activities For Families* (Notre Dame, IN: Ave Maria, 2015), "Monday of Holy Week."

CHAPTER THREE

1. Dos Santos, 156.

2. Dos Santos, 158.

3. Sister Lucia of Jesus, 126.

4. Dos Santos, 158.

5. Sister Lucia of Jesus, 126.

6. Sister Lucia of Jesus, 127.

7. Dos Santos, 158.

8. Dos Santos, 158.

9. Dos Santos, 160.

10. Dos Santos, 66–67.

11. Dos Santos, 66–67.

12. Dos Santos, 161.

13. Dos Santos, 161.

CHAPTER FOUR

1. Dos Santos, 161.

2. Cardinal Raymond Leo Burke, foreword to *Fatima For Today: The Urgent Marian Message of Hope,* by Andrew Apostoli, CFR (San Francisco: Ignatius, 2010), x.
3. "The Message of Fatima."
4. Dos Santos, 162.
5. Dos Santos, 162.
6. "The Message of Fatima," 24.
7. Dos Santos, 105.
8. Faustina Kowalska, *Divine Mercy In My Soul: The Diary of the Servant of God Sister M. Faustina Kowalska* (Stockbridge, MA: Marian, 2014), 741.
9. "The Message of Fatima," 8.
10. Mark Fellows, *Lucia's Fourth Memoir,* 162, in "Chapter 26: Letters and Memoirs (1930–1942)," *Sister Lucia: Apostle of Mary's Immaculate Heart,* http://www.srlucia.com/.
11. Dos Santos, 32.
12. Dos Santos, 105.
13. Dos Santos, 74.
14. *Sister Lucia of Jesus,* 101.
15. "The Message of Fatima," 19.
16. "The Message of Fatima," Theological Commentary, 1.
17. "The Message of Fatima," Theological Commentary, 20.
18. "The Message of Fatima," 13-VII-1917.
19. "The Message of Fatima," Sister Lucia's letter to Pope John Paul II, 12 May 1982.
20. "The Message of Fatima," 5.
21. "The Message of Fatima,", From the diary of John XXIII, 17 August 1959, final section (1).
22. "The Message of Fatima," 4.

Chapter Five
1. Pope Benedict XVI (homily, Esplanade of the Shrine of Our Lady of Fatima, May 13, 2010), 11.
2. Apostoli, *Fatima For Today,* 96.
3. Dos Santos, 35.
4. Dos Santos, 35–36.
5. Dos Santos, 128.
6. Dos Santos, 166.
7. Dos Santos, 167.
8. Dos Santos, 167.

CHAPTER SIX

1. John de Marchi, IMC, *Fatima: From the Beginning*, trans. I. M. Kingsbury (Fatima, Portugal: Missoes Consolata Fatima, 2006), 128.
2. De Marchi, *Fatima: From the Beginning*, 128.
3. De Marchi, *Fatima: From the Beginning*, 128.
4. Dos Santos, 168.
5. De Marchi, *Fatima: From the Beginning*, 128.
6. De Marchi, *Fatima: From the Beginning*, 128.
7. Dos Santos, 168.
8. Dos Santos, 170.
9. De Marchi, *From the Beginning*, 135–136.
10. Asdrubal Castello Branco and Phillip C. M. Kelly, CSC, translator's foreword to *The Crusade of Fatima: The Lady More Brilliant Than the Sun* by John De Marchi (New York: P.J. Kenedy, 1948), ix.
11. De Marchi, *From the Beginning*, 137.
12. De Marchi, *From the Beginning*, 137.
13. Fulton J. Sheen, *The World's First Love: Mary, Mother of God* (San Francisco: Ignatius, 1952), 273.
14. Dos Santos, 170.

CHAPTER SEVEN

1. "The Message of Fatima."
2. Dos Santos, 137.
3. Dos Santos, 145.
4. De Marchi, *From the Beginning*, 192.
5. John de Marchi, *The Crusade of Fatima: The Lady More Brilliant Than the Sun*, Asdrubal Castello Branco and Phillip C.M. Kelly, CSC (New York: P.J. Kenedy, 1948), 124.
6. Dos Santos, 45.
7. De Marchi, *From the Beginning*, 192.
8. Apostoli, *Fatima For Today*, 145.
9. Sister Lucia to her mother, June 11, 1930 at Tuy, Spain, convent, in *The Intimate Life of Sister Lucia* by Fr. Robert J. Fox (Waite Park, MN: Fatima Family Apostolate, 2001), 216.

CHAPTER EIGHT

1. Sister Lucia, *The Intimate Life of Sister Lucia*, 169.
2. *Intimate Life*, 183.
3. *Intimate Life*, 185.
4. *Intimate Life*, 181, 182.

5. *Intimate Life*, 179.
6. *Intimate Life*, 180.
7. *Intimate Life*, 181.
8. *Intimate Life*, 185.
9. *Intimate Life*, 313.
10. *Intimate Life*, 314.
11. *Intimate Life*, 143.
12. *Intimate Life*, 170.
13. *Intimate Life*, 216.
14. Dos Santos, 195.
15. Dos Santos, 161.
16. Apostoli, *Fatima For Today*, 151.
17. Dos Santos, 196–197.
18. Dos Santos, 197.
19. Dos Santos, 197.
20. Dos Santos, 195.
21. World Apostolate of Fatima, *Spiritual Guide for the Salvation of Souls and World Peace* (Washington, NJ: World Apostolate of Fatima, USA, 2008), 128–129.
22. Dos Santos, 199–200.
23. Apostoli, *Fatima for Today*, 162.
24. Apostoli, *Fatima for Today*, 162.
25. Dos Santos, 200.

CHAPTER NINE
1. Blessed Jacinta to Sister Lucia in "The True Story of Fatima," EWTN, http://www.ewtn.com/library/MARY/tsfatima.htm.
2 "The True Story of Fatima."
3. Cardinal Joseph Ratzinger, "Theological Commentary: An attempt to interpret the 'secret' of Fatima," in "The Message of Fatima."
4. Apostoli, *Fatima For Today*, 168.
5. Fr. Anthony Mario Martins, SJ, *Novos Documentos de Fatima* (N.p.: Oporto: 1984). English edition: *Documents on Fatima & Memoirs of Sr. Lucia* (Alexandria, SD: Fatima Family Apostolate, 1992).
6. Timothy Tindale-Robertson, *Fatima, Russia and John Paul II: How Mary Intervened to Deliver Russia from Marxist Atheism May 13, 1981–December 25, 1991*, rev. ed. (Still River, MA: Ravengate, 1998), 232–233.
7. Tindale-Robertson, 232–233.
8. Pope Paul VI, *Signum Magnum*, 8.

9. Cardinal Stanislaw Dziwisz, *A Life with Karol: My Forty-Year Friendship with the Man Who Became Pope* (New York: Image, 2008), 136.
10. John Paul II, " Act of Entrustment" (radio message, Ceremony of Veneration, Thanksgiving and Entrustment to the Virgin Mary Theotokos in the Basilica of Saint Mary Major, June 7, 1981).
11. "The Message of Fatima," 16–25.
12. "The Message of Fatima," 1.

CHAPTER TEN

1. Joseph Cacella, *Fatima and the Rosary* (New York: St. Anthony Welfare Center, 1944), 5.
2. John A. Hardon, SJ, "Our Lady of Fatima in the Light of History," John A. Hardon, SJ Archives, The Real Presence Association, http://www.therealpresence.org/archives/Mariology/Mariology_030.htm.
3. Hardon, "Our Lady of Fatima."
4. St. Alphonsus Liguori, *Glories of Mary* (New York: Redemptorist Fathers, 1927), Part V, No. 4.
5. Apostoli, *Fatima for Today*, 248.
6. *Spiritual Guide*, 128–29
7. Michelle Laque Johnson, "Our Lady Requested First Saturday Devotions – EWTN Makes It Easy!" EWTN's *WINGS Weekly E-Newsletter*, May 2, 2013.
8. Pronechen.

CHAPTER ELEVEN

1. "The Message of Fatima," 1.
2. John Paul II, "Homily at Fatima."
3. John A. Hardon, SJ Archives, "The Essential Message of Fatima," John A. Hardon, SJ Archives, The Real Presence Association, http://www.therealpresence.org/archives/Miracles/Miracles_007.htm.
4. John A. Hardon, SJ Archives, "Fatima and Miracles of Conversion," John A. Hardon, SJ Archives, The Real Presence Association, http://www.therealpresence.org/archives/Miracles/Miracles_006.htm.
5. Apostoli, *Fatima for Today*, 221
6. Apostoli, *Fatima for Today*, 221.
7. Apostoli, *Fatima for Today*, 123.
8. Americo Pablo Lopez-Ortiz, "The Message of Fatima Focuses on the Sanctification of Our Families," *Children of the Eucharist*, June 2016, http://childrenoftheeucharist.org/wp-content/uploads/2016/06/Fatima-focuses-on-the-sanctification-of-our-families.pdf.

9. Americo Pablo Lopez-Ortiz, interview by Mitch Pacwa, *EWTN Live*, EWTN, October 10, 2012.

10. John Paul II, "Homily at Fatima."

11. Benjamin Harnwell, "The Family is the Battlefield in a Great Spiritual War," *National Catholic Register,* July 13, 2015.

12. Joe Tremblay, "The 100-year test," Catholic News Agency, February 1, 2013.

13. Andrew Apostoli, CFR, in interview with the author, DATE.

14. Colin B. Donovan, STL, in interview with the author, DATE.

AFTERWORD

1. John Haffert, Meet the Witnesses (Asbury, NJ: 101 Foundation, 2002), 80.

APPENDIX A

1. From the official website for the Fatima Shrine: http://www.fatima.pt/en/pages/prayer-for the-canonization-of-francisco-and-jacinta.

2. Dos Santos, 182.

3. The Luminous Mysteries were added by Pope John Paul II in 2002 in his apostolic letter The Rosary of the Virgin Mary.

4. United States Conference of Catholic Bishops: http://www.usccb.org/prayer-and-worship/prayers-and-devotions/rosaries/how-to-pray-the-rosary.cfm.

5. "International Pilgrim Virgin Statue US Tour for Peace," Catholic Pilgrimage Sites, https://catholicpilgrimagesites.wordpress.com/2016/04/28/international-pilgrim-virgin-statue-us-tour-for-peace/.

6. *Intimate Life,* 59.

7. John Paul II, "Homily at Fatima."

8. See http://www.vatican.va/roman_curia/congregations/cfaith/documents/rc_con_cfaith_doc_20000626_message-fatima_en.html.

APPENDIX B

1. John A. Hardon, SJ, "The Doctrinal Message of Fatima," John A. Hardon, SJ Archives, The Real Presence Association, http://www.therealpresence.org/archives/Church_Dogma/Church_Dogma_041.htm.

With a grateful heart to all who have guided me, prayed for me, and loved me throughout my life: my family and friends, especially my parents, Eugene Joseph and Alexandra Mary Cooper, and my brothers and sisters, Alice Jean, Gene, Gary, Barbara, Tim, Michael, and David—I am eternally indebted.

My children have always been my utmost vocation. I love you, Justin, Chaldea, Jessica, Joseph, and Mary-Catherine! And to my grandson, Shepherd James—I love you, too! My husband, Dave, the wind beneath my wings, thank you for your love and support!

I owe a special thanks to Fr. Andrew Apostoli, CFR, for his wonderful foreword and his friendship and prayers. And to my dear "Sisters in Christ" for their many prayers that continually help to sustain me in my work and ministry. I am grateful for the intercession of three of my dear saint friends in heaven: Fr. John A. Hardon, SJ, Fr. Bill C. Smith, and St. Teresa of Calcutta (in my heart she remains "Mother Teresa")!

Heartfelt thanks to Heidi Hess Saxton, Louise Pare, Katie Carroll, and the wonderful team at Servant for their partnership in getting this book out to you! Loving prayers for all who are connected through my books, talks, and pilgrimages—thank you for joining me in prayer on the spectacular journey that leads to eternal life! And, of course, I also thank my guardian angel, my wonderful personal assistant!

ABOUT THE AUTHOR

Donna-Marie Cooper O'Boyle is a Catholic wife, mother, grandmother, pilgrimage host, and a bestselling and award-winning author of more than twenty books. She is also an award-winning journalist, speaker, catechist, and retreat leader. She is the EWTN television host of *Everyday Blessings for Catholic Moms, Catholic Moms Café,* and *Feeding Your Family's Soul.* Donna-Marie enjoyed a decade-long friendship with St. Teresa of Calcutta, and received spiritual direction from Servant of God John A. Hardon, SJ. She has received apostolic blessings from St. John Paul II and Pope Emeritus Benedict XVI as well as a special blessing from St. John Paul II on Donna-Marie's writing on Mother Teresa. In 2009 she was listed as one of the "Top Ten Most Fascinating Catholics" in *Faith and Family Live.* Her memoir is entitled *The Kiss of Jesus: How Mother Teresa and the Saints Helped Me to Discover the Beauty of the Cross.* Learn more about Donna-Marie and her ministry and pilgrimages at www. donnacooperoboyle.com and www.feedingyourfamilysoul.com.